"SURVIVAL WAS FOR ME"

by

DUNCAN WILSON

*Is an account of life as an ordinary
soldier in Japanese Prisoner of War Camps
in Singapore and Thailand 1942 - 1945.
A story of death with no glory, no tears,
but all sweat and starvation for 3 $^1/_2$ years.*

"SURVIVAL WAS FOR ME"

by

DUNCAN WILSON

Royal Corps of Signals

PUBLISHED BY DUNCAN WILSON
in conjunction with
GC BOOKS LTD, WIGTOWN

Published in Scotland
By Duncan Wilson in conjunction with
GC BOOKS LTD, 6 SOUTH MAIN STREET
WIGTOWN, SCOTLAND

Copyright (C) 1991 by Duncan Wilson
Catherine Street,
Gatehouse of Fleet, Kirkcudbrightshire
Scotland

Printed in the UK by Billings & Son Ltd.,
Hylton Road, Worcester. WR2 5JU

ISBN 1 872350 20 8

CONTENTS

Index to plates

This book is dedicated to

G

and

STEPHANIE

CHAPTER ONE

THE HOLIDAY CAMP

When I left the train at the seaside resort of Prestatyn, in North Wales, in answer to my call up papers for the forces I intended to go to the Station Hotel and have a last Civilian Meal before being swallowed up by the Army.

However, it was not to be. I was intercepted on the platform by a Regimental Sergeant Major. "Are you for the Army depot?" was the brusque question, "Yes but" I said, and then realised my excuse that I wanted to go for a meal would not be believed. It would be more likely I had cold feet and was off home on the next train.

I was bundled into a transit wagon along with all the other poor devils destined for Army Service and were soon passing through the gates of the camp under the sign 'Welcome to Prestatyn Holiday Camp' emblazoned over a large archway.

We were taken through the usual routine of being documented and kitted out with Army uniforms. There appeared to be three sizes, big, little and tiny. The last issue was a piece of brown paper and a length of string. This was to parcel up all our civilian clothes and the Army kindly paid the postage to send them to our homes. I had a feeling it would be a long time before I needed them again.

This handing in of my civilian clothes seemed like the end of a chapter in my life. From then on I belonged to the Army and not to me. I was not to know that in two months I would be on the high seas heading for I knew not where. That I would lose more than half my good Army friends by slow and painful starvation. That we would be the victims of three and a half years of forced labour, culminating in our digging our own intended tombs. Only the dropping of the Atomic Bomb saved us from being herded into our own made graves .

The Japanese Guards had told us when we were digging holes in the hillside "English soldiers land Singapore - you go in tunnel and we throw bomb in - all prisoners gone."

The first week at Prestatyn we were not allowed out of the camp and the barrack huts were only warmed with a coal fired stove with was either red hot or had gone out. This was the early part of September 1940. We dug trenches in the sand dunes every Saturday morning and these were filled by the sand being blown back and filling them up sometimes within hours. We did sentry duty in or "on" these trenches every dusk and dawn in case the Germans decided on an invasion via the North Wales coast.

As a married man my pay to draw was around seven shillings and sixpence per week. Usually by Wednesday I had exhausted my pay and if I had some stamps sent from home I would wait by the stamp machine and flog a couple of stamps to the men so that I could have a cup of tea in the canteen.

I learnt early, the more devious methods in the Army. I was detailed to help in the Quartermasters Stores. An officer arrived during the day and did a spot check on the various stores in stock. We were one telephone short according to our records.

The Q.M. said that this phone was in another hut. As soon as the Inspector had gone through the front door I was told to take a phone to the other hut and make sure I got there before the Inspector and put it with the other ones to be counted in that hut.

The missing telephone was probably installed in some local landlady's house in Prestatyn .

Every fortnight a fresh intake of recruits from all over Britain would arrive at the Prestatyn Camp for basic training. We who had been in the Army for a full fortnight considered ourselves almost as "old soldiers". Many of these recruits had never been away from home before. I had never realised how true it was that the average man from South of Watford Gap, had never been north of Watford Gap. They cam from all manner of different social classes but most mixed well and made friends regardless of their respective backgrounds. The Army uniform is a great leveller particularly before the clothes had time to assimilate your character .

After a few weeks we moved into Chalets in another part of the camp. These had been occupied by holiday makers until the end of the Summer season. These were of course normally used during the Summer and it was now near Christmas. We had a very heavy snow storm during one night and it piled the snow high against the chalets doors., We opened the door and faced a wall of snow six feet high. In a few seconds it fell into the Chalets onto the bunks and floor.

The Winter had now set in. The Chalets were never meant to house people in Winter and we had to pile our great coats on top of the inadequate bedding provided.

When we had Passed Out in whatever trade in the Royal Signals Corps we were to be put into, we were transferred to the Holding Battallion in Colwyn Bay.

I cannot say with truth that what I learned at Prestatyn Camp really served much towards my survival. Now at Colwyn Bay we were supposed to be soldiers.

There was no camp, as such, there. We were billeted in various hotels and boarding houses which had been requisitioned by the War Office. The rooms were bereft of all furniture and carpets. The Company Office was in a private hotel, the Mess Room was a garage and we had lectures and physical training in the Pier Ballroom. There were fireplaces in most rooms where we were billeted but we had no fuel allowance.

Whilst I was on a fatigue peeling potatoes at the Mess someone reported they had lost a wallet. There was a hue and cry, all exits were closed and everyone was lined up to be searched. The wallet was not discovered but we were all wearing dungarees with large blouses and every man was found to have coal secreted in the jackets. This was intended for us to have one room in the billet with a fire. We lost the coal but we were not charged with any offence.

I had a standing invitation to have a meal once a week with a friend of mine in Colwyn Bay. The husband asked me what I thought of the meat. Rationing was very severe and I was lucky to be served with meat. I said it was very nice. He said "I get it from my garageman in the town. He lets me have some each week." I refrained from comment but the garage happened to be used as our Mess room so our cooks must have been flogging our rations to him.

I was twice waiting on the station at Colwyn Bay with a draft going abroad, as Reserve, in case anyone was missing before the train left, but no one was missing. I went back to the camp and handed the Tropical Kit back to the Quartermasters Stores.

The thought of what was going to happen to me did not really matter so much as 'Will I get a letter from home soon' - 'Will I have enough money to buy a pint tonight'.

After being on the two earlier drafts as waiting man and in both cases no-one failed to appear, I stayed with the Unit at Colwyn Bay. I was again put on a draft, which according to the bar girls in the local pubs, who usually seemed to know before us, was destined for the Far East. In view of the fact that we drew Tropical Kit and Topee from the stores they were probably right.

After five or six inoculations we were given a weekends leave and were to depart the following Thursday. On the Wednesday night most of the men who were going went out, and after the pubs closed we went to a dance on the Pier. The regulations were that no military personnel were to be on the streets after eleven o'clock at night. We expected the Military Police to be waiting for us as it was midnight before the dance ended. We made no effort to escape and anyway the road had a steep bank on one side and the sea on the other. Out came the notebooks and the usual warning that we were supposed to be in our Billets by eleven. There were perhaps twenty men in our party and just two redcaps (Military Police) who carefully made a list of our unit, name, rank and regimental number. We were warned that we would be on a charge the following morning. One man said "Sorry mate we will be leaving on the train at six in the morning." After asking everyone and receiving the same reply they tore the pages out of their books, wished us luck and we went on our way back to our various Billets.

The following morning we assembled on the parade ground and marched to the station and entrained after a double check that all were present and no-one had slipped away. Our destination was a secret but we arrived in the Docks in Liverpool and boarded a Canadian Pacific boat called the "Duchess of York". At this time we had seen from Colwyn Bay almost every night the terrible bombing of Liverpool Docks. We stayed in port all that night and not a single bomber came over, probably because it was a very windy night. One of the mens father worked on the Docks and realised his son may be on this ship. The two were delighted to see each other and the only ones out of all aboard to say a personal and sad goodbye. It was to be three and a half weary years before any of us saw Britain again.

We as a Signal Unit were a comparative small group and we were fortunate in being allocated to third class cabins with bunks. The majority of the troops were allocated space below decks and the conditions were awful and got worse when we arrived in the tropics. We were joined as we went North by more ships from Glasgow and included Destroyers and the battleship "Nelson". We were told that there were some fifty ships in the convoy.

After a few days we were mustered on deck for physical exercise which included jumping up and down. This was soon abandoned when three or four men were knocked unconscious by hitting parts of the ships structure with their heads! In order to get some exercise we ran around the ships deck. The monotony of life aboard was boring and I was thankful I had brought a pack of cards with me. We spent hours playing Brag or solo whist and the same money was going round and round as we were not getting paidout during the early part of the voyage. I played all day and until well after midnight only missing the odd hand to collect a meal from the Mess-Deck.

This ship we were sailing in was a medium sized ship which normally worked in the regular route to Canada and back. Its official title was The Duchess of York but according to the crew it was known as The Drunken duchess because of its erratic behaviour in a rough sea.

We sailed away to somewhere near the Azores through mostly calm seas. One of the Signals Corporals was sea sick on a calm sea on the first night at sea. He was ill for the whole of the voyage of some twelve weeks.

Throughout the voyage until we reached Bombay the whole convoy was sailing first to the right and then to the left in formation with each ship having to keep at the same distance from each other. This meant that we were restricted to the speed equal to the slowest in the whole convoy. Occasionally the alarms would sound and every man had to don his lifebelt and parade on the deck which he had been assigned to in emergency drills. All the ships would scatter until the stand down was given. This meant that the faster ships had to sail slowly until the slower boats had reformed within the convoy. As we got further from Europe the Alerts became less frequent. Occasionally the battleship would put on speed and go forward to investigate an alarm. The destroyers would also break convoy and sail at the edge of the whole fleet.

We did not know where we were going and speculation ran high. Would it be South Africa or maybe India but always we decided it would most likely be Singapore.

As we sailed off the coast of Africa, the air in the cabins became almost unbearably hot and stuffy. It was even worse in the holds where the majority of the troops slept. The ship was never intended to work in the tropics and had no air conditioning.

Many of the troops who were supposed to sleep below decks in the holds slept instead on the upper decks or wherever the temperature was lowered by the ships movement. Some nights if I was unable to get to sleep I went to the stern of the ship where I could be alone for a while and I was fascinated as I watched the shining sulphur sea glisten in the darkness as the propellers churned up the water below me. Our ship was of course completely blacked out and could not show any light visible from outside and it was not easy to find a way through the passages and along the deck to the stern of the ship. However, during the beautiful moonlit nights I had been going to this haven and knew my way.

On one particular morning I had gone to the stern for some fresh air about four o'clock and stood leaning against the rails directly over the propeller. I could feel the sea spray on my body and face and was fascinated by the continuous rythmic hum of the engines, the beating noise of the water and the foam and fluorescent lights dancing in the spume. We were, as we had been all the voyage, keeping a zig zag course of steering. Suddenly as I stared down in the black darkness the light from the water reflected on something only a few yards above me and the pattern of our wash appeared to change. I looked upwards and saw to my horror the bow of a ship actually over the top of where I was standing and I could even see ropes dangling from the ships rails.

I was almost petrified and thought "What is the drill for such an occasion?". My first thought was to alert the Bridge, but how could I find my way to the Bridge in the dark? When I again looked upwards there was no sign or sight of any ship, but the wake crossed our bows, the crisis seemed to be over. I felt no-one would believe my story and as the danger was over I settled down to enjoy the soothing rhythm of the propellers and the swish of the sea. I realised how near to death and disaster I, and all aboard the ship had been. I thanked God and slowly made my way back to my cabin, turned into my bunk still rather shaken by my experience. No-one appeared to be awake to tell my story to so I went straight to sleep. I awoke later in the morning and thought about the previous nights experience. I decided no-one would believe my story and so I never mentioned it until a year or so had gone by.

We had now been at sea for several weeks without ever having set foot on dry land. The nights and days passed slowly with nothing to do but play cards or watch the porpoise and flying fish and whales.

We arrived in a large tropical bay with trees coming right down to the shore. Many ships were anchored and lighters were shuttling from ship to shore. This was Freetown, Sierra Leone, which in those days did not have docking facilities.

Our ship was quickly surrounded by "BUM BOATS" crewed by the local people and loaded with all sorts of carved elephants, bananas and other local fruit. Necklaces made from all sorts of animal and fish teeth .

All these boatmen swarmed around our ship and threw onto the decks light-weight baskets attached to a piece of string, the other end of which they kept hold themselves. We aboard the ship were invited to put money in the basket to buy whatever article or fruit the native was offering. This was then lowered down to the boat and the article hauled back up by the buyer, and if the seller was lucky his basket was thrown back to his boat.

In some instances as the basket was passing a lower port hole an arm would stretch out and grab the bananas or whatever from the basket. This barter went on for some time until those willing to buy had run out of money (we had not been paid since leaving England).

The boatmen then started to offer money for Army clothing. Shirts, shorts, vests and other clothing of Army issue was seen passing the lower decks by our Officers. This could not be allowed to continue. Efforts were made to warn the boatmen away but to no avail. As a last resort our crew turned the powerful fire hoses on them. They retreated only as far as the hose could reach ready to return if it was turned off .

We stayed in Freetown for about 36 hours. The whole ship became like an oven without the movement of air circulated through the cabins when we were moving. We sailed away the next day and the convoy reformed. Still we had no confirmation of out destination.

A little light relief was provided at the Crossing the Equator ceremony. A small pool was constructed on the deck and the various characters were played by sailors. Everyone received a ducking which was more than welcome in the heat of the day. Everyone was given a certificate to say that they could pass through the dateline in future free of hindrance .

By now some of the ships in the convoy had been left behind at various points nearest to their destination. We were now given to understand we would be calling at Capetown and staying for four days to replenish food and fuel stocks. We would be allowed ashore for one and a half days each so that there would always be about a quarter of troops aboard at any one time. There was a sea mist which hung over the sea as we neared Capetown. The mist seemed to lower and suddenly I saw Table top Mountain clearly in the distance but the buildings were still hidden by the mist. The city of Capetown soon came fully into view and looked very inviting. It was great to think that within hours we would be walking on dry land. We had now been aboard the ship for nine or ten weeks without setting foot on the shore and we were as excited as schoolboys on end of term day.

Two friends and myself decided to go into Capetown together. We made our minds up that we would not accept any hospitality but discover Capetown for ourselves. After window shopping for a while we went into Woolworths. We of course had our Army uniforms on. It was not long before we were approached by three women and asked if we would accept some sweets as we were opposite the sweet counters .

We agreed and were presented with a pound of each of three kinds of sweets and some cigarettes in fifty packets. They then asked us if we would like to go back to their house by the sea and have lunch with them. We hesitated in view of what we had agreed before about hospitality. The women said they would leave us to talk it over and they would wait outside for our verdict. We decided to accept their generous offer. They had a vary large car and the six of us drove to a seaside resort near Capetown where they lived.

We had a very good lunch and then spent the afternoon on the beautiful beach. The husband of the owner of the house joined us for tea and invited us to go with them to a nightclub out in the bush. This sounded great and we readily accepted and were taken to a place about twenty miles outside Capetown called The Blue Moon. The odd thing was that two of our hosts were German refugees and the third was the wife of the houseowner .

They were older than us but we had a lot of fun. Some of our own Officers arrived but we managed not to meet. We were supposed to be back aboard the ship by midnight and the time was getting near when we should have to leave to be back in time. Our host said "As soon as your Officers leave, we will leave and I guarantee you will be back on the ship before them". He had a large Mercedes car and the roads were long and straight. We did get back before the Officers, but we had our names taken to be on a charge the next day for overstaying our leave. However, as the Officers knew we had seen them arrive back after us, we heard no more. The same people took us out again the next day and as we boarded the ship they gave each of us a sack full of oranges to take aboard.

We sailed away from Capetown early the next morning having taken on provisions. The food on the voyage from Liverpool had been, to put it mildly, indifferent. When we left England eggs were very scarce and we rarely had them served for breakfast back home, but for the past month we were presented with a bowl of boiled eggs every morning and about twenty per cent of them were either stale or stinking rotten and not fit to eat. So many men had tasted them before realising that they were bad that it became the custom as soon as the orderly put them down, to pass the dish down the table and the man nearest the porthole emptied them into the sea.

Whilst at sea we had to mount guard over the entrance to the cold store. It came to my turn and I asked if I could have a look round with one of the Stewards. There must have been thousands and thousands of eggs when we sailed as there were still complete alleyways of stacks of them, and yet we had eaten and thrown away a few thousand of them each day.

I was probably only in the store for twenty minutes, but about an hour after I came out my earlobes swelled up with chilblains even though we were in the tropics.

The next stop was Bombay and most of us managed to get ashore for about three hours. We had been accompanied by a destroyer from Capetown and the rest of the convoy had gone elsewhere, but we still kept to a zig-zag course. We left Bombay in the evening, and as soon as we were out to sea, it was full steam ahead and the poor old ship rattled and shuddered and by dawn we were on our own and there was no doubt we were going in a straight line for somewhere and by now the destination appeared to be Singapore. We all did a watch or two submarine spotting but still found time to play cards.

CHAPTER TWO

DESTINATION SINGAPORE

Our arrival in Singapore on the troopship Duchess of York on the 23rd March 1941 was greeted by a torrential downpour and, as we paraded onshore at Keppel Harbour Quay, the welcome was not of the best. We had been at sea for twelve weeks and had only been ashore twice. Trucks and drivers from the camp at which the Royal Signals were stationed met us on the quayside and we were soon whisked away to a tented camp in a clearing in a rubber plantation some four miles from the docks.

We were marched to the Quartermasters store to collect beds and bedding and one tent to each six men. Pitching tents was something we had never done or seen done but after a while we discovered we were very short of tent pegs. We took the easy way out and strolled past the tents which had ben up for sometime and pulled up a peg which looked as if it would not cause the immediate collapse of the tent and eventually had enough pegs to make our tents safer than the ones which had been up some time.

About four hours after leaving the docks we were allowed a break for a mug of tea. This was the first drink for about six hours and in addition to not being used to the hundred degree temperature we were not used to work of any kind after being cooped up aboard ship for twelve weeks. We now had to fit the pieces of bed together. These consisted of an iron headpiece, two pieces of wire mesh frame and a foot end. Unfortunately these had probably been made locally by hand on the basis of one man one bed. To assemble them was a matter of trying to get four pieces which fitted and involved changing various parts with each other and working on a trial and error basis until one bed had the right combination.

Mattresses were cotton covers filled with coconut fibre about a metre square and two to each bed. There was also an issue of two sheets and a mosquito net. This was real luxury. The first chance to have a wash was around five o'clock. After our twelve weeks on the ship it was marvellous to have a shower out in the warm air with rain water and not sea water. My whole outlook changed and I realised I could perhaps get some enjoyment out of life in this glorious climate and country.

Parade for a meal with mess tins and mugs was at 18.00 hours. The meal, served from a field kitchen, was a sort of stew and I think contained a proportion of old Yak. The meal was taken into a mess tent and we had our first chance to talk to the "Old Sweats" who had been here about three months. It was easy to tell the new intake as it was obvious from our pale faces we were new. They wanted to know the latest news from England and which towns had been bombed etc. However, we had received no mail and apart from a ships bulletin each day we had no news that was not twelve weeks old. The mood changed and we were regaled with horror stories of life in the jungle. According to these first hand accounts, we were likely to see at least one tiger in our first week. Frogs would invade our tents as soon as it rained, bed bugs would prevent us sleeping and every mosquito bite would result in Malaria or Dengue Fever. Our chances of contracting Dysentery were about 50-50. We were advised to empty our shoes of scorpions and look under the bed for snakes.

Filled with all these horror stories and a few pints of beer from the canteen we wandered away to try and find our correct tent. We had no lights but the tents were pitched in a clearing and it was a beautiful moonlit night. The next task was how to get under a mosquito net without taking a load of mosquitos with you, and when you had got in and tucked all the sides in, how did you know that the buzzing close to you was inside or outside the net? After such a hard day I was soon asleep. I awoke in the early hours of the morning feeling awful. The tent appeared to be going round and my feet seemed to be much higher than my head. I struggled with the net and managed to get my feet on the floor and found that the iron legs at the head end of my bed had sunk into the ground and my feet were indeed much higher than my head. I decided the best plan was to change ends and to sleep feet to head and my weight, I hoped would sink the foot end and level me out. By morning the bed was level with all four legs deep in the ground. Dawn is always at around six o'clock and I was glad to get a shower after the sticky heat of the night which left a moist patch of sweat on the sheets and the net very damp. Parade after breakfast was taken by a Senior Officer who explained that until we were accustomed to the climate there would only be light work for us.

This was soon proved to be totally untrue as a party of us, all from the new intake, were taken in a truck to the docks to uplift all the equipment belonging to the Signals and bring it back into the camp. It was packed in large crates and wooden boxes, and we had to load and unload these without any mechanical help.

We had about an hours break at midday and then were back at the docks for a further load. So the "light work" lasted from 9.00 a.m. to 5.00 p.m. with only an hours break for a cup of tea and a round of bread with a pilchard at midday. This was then considered light work. We wondered what hard work would be like. Little did I realise that these days were idleness compared to what we would suffer later in our service.

I had not been alone for twelve weeks and so I used to take a walk down to the nearest village and really enjoyed just the very fact of being alone for a little while and I loved the noise and the atmosphere of the tropical mights.

We were all Royal Signals at this camp and after a week or so of general work sorting out our stores some of us were posted to Signal Offices. I was one of half a dozen men sent to work at Fort Canning which was the headquarters of South East Asia Command. We worked in eight hour shifts day and night. This I liked because we could go out in the day some days and nights other times. We lived in a hut on the side of a hill overlooking a large part of Singapore. Our mess room was near and we were served by Chinese boys. We had a choice of foods and iced drinks and this proved to be the best Billet I had throughout my service in Malaya. Tea was brought to our bedside at seven in the morning and when we came back from having a wash and shave our beds would be made ready for inspection at eleven o'clock. Then the Indian Orderly would remake our beds ready for sleep. If we had been on night duty we would finish at 6.00 a.m.and sleep till twelve and probably go in a party down into Singapore town.

If we had any washing the Indians would take it in the morning and bring it back before the evening. It would be pressed and if you paid, they would clean all your buttons and lay the clothes out ready for you to put on. We were on the telephone switchboard at Fort Canning and were left alone, and as long as the job was done and the switchboard manned no-one seemed to bother. Occasionally we took it in turns to have an extra day off, and as long as we kept out of the camp no-one noticed.

The shorts which we had been issued with in Britain were wide legged and reached to the knee. If you were out in town or out of camp the rule was that shorts, which were let down by unfastening a button at each side of the leg, and the legs came down to about mid-calf, had to be let down so that the bare knees were covered and the mosquitos could not officially bite you after 6.00 p.m. Everyone disliked this garment, but the only alternative was long drill trousers which were smart but very hot to wear in the daytime. We were also issued with a tin of anti-mosquito cream which was supposed to act as a deterrent. However, it always appeared to attract them and they loved it so we stopped using it.

As an ordinary Signalman (married) my pay was about six Malayan dollars. A half pint bottle of beer cost 52 cents and a whisky cost 48 cents, so we could seldom paint the town red. One night out and that was it for the week. A rickshaw to town from the barracks could cost from 25 cents to a dollar. Sometimes, if we had spent all our money, it meant either a long walk or a rickshaw to the barrack gates and a quick jump out before it stopped and then a run past the sentry on the gate and hope the Rickshaw Wallah did not recognise you next time you were in town. We had great fun in the street markets bargaining with the Chinese who were always ready to meet banter with more banter and throughout my stay I found the Chinese particularly friendly. We also frequented the two fun-fairs and the open air theatre.

We also had the Union Jack Club in Singapore town. This was manned by volunteers who I understood, were wives of English, Dutch and Chinese businessmen living in Singapore. It was only open to members of the armed forces. The food and drinks there were cheaper than the Cafes in town and they held Housey Housey sessions once a week when the prize could be up to 100 dollars. We were always welcome there even though we had little money to spend, we could go into the Club and sit around without spending, apart from a cup of tea .

At this time the war in the Far East against Japan had not begun and although we had little doubt that sooner or later we would be involved we did not really worry about it. We were well fed and well looked after at Fort Canning and had Indian servants to look after us in the barracks and Chinese cooks and waiters to get our meals. We were living the life that was typical of our troops in any part of the Empire before 1939. I had been used to working long hours in civilian life in town and an hour each night and morning travelling to work. This life was idleness to me. Nevertheless we had alot of fun and spent hours of spontaneous discussion of politics, religion, our home lives, our wives and girl friends. So many different sections of life were represented by the Regular Army, the Conscripts and the Volunteers. There was very strong feeling on most subjects but apart from the occasional verbal flare-up there was no violence and many of those who had just been arguing vehemently would be all off down town in the evening together. If an argument appeared to be culminating in an agreement there was always one of us who would be prepared to change our opinion to keep the argument lively, as devils advocate.

I felt guilty about living in this easy cushioned life in a most beautiful country, as, when I left England, I could see from our base in Colwyn Bay the German bombers knocking hell out of Liverpool and we were on dawn and dusk alert in case the Germans invaded the North Wales coast!

Here in Singapore the skies were clear of bombers, we had no air raid sirens and life for most people living there was almost unaffected by the european war. I often thought of those I loved living in Britain and what they were suffering, and many times I wished I could return home and face what may come there.

There came a request from the Signal Office at Kuala Lumpur for a switchboard operator to work in their office for a temporary posting. It always seemed to be me who got these odd jobs and had been so since I joined up. I had decided from the first day in the Army that I would not try and deliberately avoid a posting or a fatigue so I was quite keen to go up country. I adopted this attitude and for the next three and a half years, sometimes I won and sometimes I lost.

In some ways I was glad to break the monotony at Fort Canning but sorry to leave the men I had worked and played with and we did have the Fort Canning job "sewn-up".

CHAPTER THREE

UP COUNTRY

I was issued with a third class warrant for the midnight express to Kuala Lumpur. The Duty Driver to take me to Singapore station was a friend and we left the barracks early and had a few drinks at the Union Jack Club with some of the usual crowd and about half past eleven I made my way onto the platform. The sight was amazing, the whole platform seemed to be covered with bundles and people, and it was difficult to distinguish the people from the bundles.

There appeared to be people from every nationality from the Far East and India. I wondered why were all these people, men, women and children all setting off at midnight with their bundles of clothing and baskets and bags, with goodness knows what in them.

I sat on my Kit Bag on the huge platform and felt like a little boy lost. I appeared to be the only European travelling on the midnight express. Do all Singapore businessmen have so much time available to them there is no necessity for them to travel at night? Even in a small country like Britain I often saved time by going to London from Manchester or to Glasgow by midnight train.

I was of course dressed in the usual walking out dress and the heat was terrific even though it was midnight. Eventually the huge engine drew into the platform amidst a cloud of smoke and steam and all the people and bundles started to move toward the train. I too had everything I possessed in my Haversack, large back-pack and side valise and Kit Bag. I found a carriage with only a few people in and settled down for the long hot journey and I hoped to get some sleep. There were no drinks or food on the train I had to manage with a drink from my water bottle and hope I could make it last for the journey. On the other side of the passage sat an old Chinaman and I noticed his nails were about three inches long. He must have realised I did not have anything to eat and with sign language offered me a banana and then a hard boiled egg. I was very grateful and sorry I could not speak to him .

The train stopped a few times to pick up timber logs to fire the engine and at one or two stations to take on water and more passengers. It had been a very dark night and I was sorry to be passing through all this jungle and see nothing of it. The dawn broke and I watched the sun rising and shining through the trees. It was a gorgeous sight .

I was thinking as we rushed through the countryside what would I give to be back and what the hell was I doing on a train miles from home and not knowing when, if ever, I would get home. We came to a clearing in the jungle, there was an old man working in amongst his crops, a woman was milking a goat and two children were happily playing with a dog. Who, I thought, was better off, the man with all his family and home around him, or me miles away from all those I cared for. At that moment I had no doubt who was better off but heavens knows what he and his family went through after the Japanese invasion .

The train thundered on through the night with a hoot and a bang and a rattling of crossings and points and an occasional stop at a station. The journey had now become interesting as the sun rose higher in the sky and looking out of the window one could see people starting work in the paddy fields and the rubber tappers collecting their little pots of latex from each tree, pouring it into a little bucket. Bullocks harnessed to carts with their large wheels trundling along the dusty roads and completely ignoring the belching steam and smoke from our modern form of transport .

At last we drew into Kuala Lumpur station and I said goodbye to my Chinese benefactor. I took great care in shaking his hand as I was afraid of getting entangled in those long finger nails. I was met at the station by a driver and wagon from the camp I was destined to.

This was an Attap Hutted camp some two miles from the

town centre and on the banks of the river. Here I was glad to meet up with some of th men with whom I had been on the same troopship. I took up my post on the telephone exchange which was at a large school which had been taken over as a Forward Headquarters for Malaya. The routine was similar to the job at Fort Canning and just as boring. The camp being near the river there were quite a few snakes around the huts but they were mostly harmless.

A night exercise for the unit was scheduled for all troops except those on duty during the day. As I was on Signal duty during that day I was put onto Main Gate Guard with the rest of the men from my shift to be on duty all night. Just after midnight, a Rickshaw appeared out of the gloom containing a very voluble Sergeant Major who demanded we allow the Rickshaw Wallah take him through the gates and to his quarters. The rule was that no unauthorised person should enter the confines of the camp.

Sergeant Major or not we were sticking to the rules and enjoying it. Every time he tried to dismount the Rickshaw Puller lifted the shafts and he fell back in the seat. If the puller does not want you to get out, it is very difficult to get out. The Rickshaw man demanded "You pay - I let him off". The Sergeant told us to pay him. "How much?", "Five Dollars" said the rickshaw man. "Where from" we asked. "K.L. to Essy Camp. Five Dollars". After much argument we settled for one dollar and the Sergeant pulled a dollar from his pocket and paid up. The Rickshaw man promptly dropped the shafts to the ground to pocket his dollar. The Sergeant was leaning forward in the seat and as the shafts dropped he slowly rolled forward and fell in a heap on the road. He was very drunk and we half carried him into the Guardroom and put him in the cell. He awoke about three hours later and threatened us with court martial and other dire consequences if we did not release him at once. We escorted him back to his quarters. Shortly afterwards the Duty Officer came round and the Exercise Convoy returned. The incident meant that those who were on the Guard were not put on any extra duties in case we told the Officer of the little fracas at the Main Gate Guardroom. Blackmail was quite legitimate in the circumstances .

The sick man I had stood in for at Kuala Lumpur returned to duty and I was sent back to Singapore. I again travelled on the midnight train and was met at Singapore station by the same driver who took me to the station on my way up country. I settled back in the huts at Fort Canning and resumed duty at the Headquarters Far East as before going to K.L.

It was back to the old routine of haggling at the market, going to the cinema at the Cathy, visiting the New World Amusement Park or coffee at the Union Jack Club. Other ranks were not allowed at such hallowed places as Raffles or any of the hotels in Singapore, and apart from one or two good ladies who served us with teas at the Union Jack Club, we had virtually no contact with Europeans who were not with the Army.

There was a very charming Chinese lady who was a voluntary worker at the Club and she was always very cheerful and welcoming. The rest of the Europeans in Singapore would go out of their way to ignore the man in Army uniform. The first time I realised this was a few days after we arrived in Singapore and went to the cinema. We were shown to our seats in the middle of a row and had to pass some Europeans. They were obviously reluctant to let us past, and I was shocked to overhear them saying to each other, should they leave. They decided they would leave, and leave they did. That was my first encounter with Singapore Colonials.

More Signals personnel were expected in Singapore and we were told we would be leaving shortly for Kuala Lumpur. We had recently received delivery of some very heavy four wheel drive Marmon trucks. Our section were allocated four of these vehicles and they were loaded with cases of equipment like radios, telephone switchboards, linesmens tools, telephone wire and all manner of useful and useless equipment.

We set off in high spirits hoping that it would be less monotonous in Kuala Lumpur than in Singapore. We were in convoy, which in the Army means each vehicle is to be a set distance behind the next one, and this distance is supposed to maintained uphill and downhill. Also accompanying the convoy were two despatch riders on motorcycles and two Ford V8 Personnel Carriers. Once we had crossed the bridge from Singapore and arrived in Johore Bahru, the roads became rough and narrower than the Singapore roads.

The big Marmon wagons were much larger than most wagons in use in Malaya at that time and consequently the local population was terrified when they saw us approaching. As we neared an ox-cart, the driver would take one look at the size of our vehicles and drive off the highway either into the forest or any opening available. The oxen then panicked and often the last we saw of them was bolting uncontrollable into the plantations or forest. There were a few cars on the roads but alot of bicycles. Most of these were laden with baskets of produce, chickens and piglets and some had small trailers fastened to the back. The Pandemonium caused by our appearance with these huge trucks was hilarious to us as we looked out from the back of our trucks to see men chasing pigs which had escaped from the baskets, chicken flying through the air and Yak carts wedged between the trees.

The journey to Kuala Lumpur is about 450 miles from Singapore so we needed to find somewhere to be able to get the convoy off the road and away from any habitation for a night stop. When we halted the only sound besides the jungle noises was the beating of drums from first one direction and then another. I presumed that the natives were telling each other about our arrival.

As it was so dark, the Commander decided we would go in the Personnel trucks and try and find somewhere to eat. We found a small village which boasted a small tea house. Our party was sixty strong and we ordered chicken soup, and within a quarter of an hour we were enjoying the soup although it was very weak chicken wise. I do not know how, but the owner managed to cook enough rice and chicken for all of us in half an hour. So expecting to serve probably half a dozen villages with coffee or tea, to cater for sixty meals was magic. He told us he knew from the drums that we were in the area.

I did my turn of Guard Duty from midnight to two o'clock and it was interesting to note that the drums were very busy on my first hour but they gradually closed down and were silent. The only noises were now of the wold animals, birds and insects which kept their chorus going all night.

We travelled all the next day through beautiful country and it was fascinating to see the activity and the children running around. At about seven in the evening, we arrived at an Australian Army camp. The Officer went to get permission to use their vehicle park for the night. We were immediately surrounded by the Australian soldiers and invited to go with them to their mess hut and have a meal. Men were queueing with their mess tins to collect their meal, but as soon as we walked in we were welcome and they insisted that we take their mess tins and have a meal and they could get more cooked for themselves when we had had our fill. It was the best meal we had for months and we expressed our thanks to the Aussies.

We were invited to go back to the mess tent in about an hour and it would be rearranged to become the canteen. We had a shower and changed and were duly welcomed back by the aussies. One of our party went to the bar to get drinks, but was told to go and sit down and sure enough the drinks were on our hosts, and all through the evening the British were not allowed to buy drinks. By eleven o'clock the tables were still filled with pints of beer and so the Aussie Officer came onto the stage and said he hoped that we had enjoyed ourselves and declared the canteen would remain open until midnight. We had all had a great night and the aussies entertained us with an impromptu stage show and lots of "Waltzing Matilda" type songs.

We staggered back to our trucks in the compound where we were to spend the night in the trucks, and were met by our Sergeant Major who detailed, in a rather incoherent voice, who was to do guard duty on the trucks through the night. It was fortunate that he dispensed with the usual Guard Parade and just detailed us for each two hour stint. I did the first two hours and had to wake the next man at 2 o'clock. I found him lying naked on his blanket in the truck and with alot of shaking and talking I eventually found him his hat and rifle. and he promised to go out on the guard as soon as he was dressed. He was a regular Army soldier and well knew all the rules so I thought he would sober up and be out in a few minutes. I went to my truck and fell asleep but later woke up and needed to relieve myself. The moon had now come out and as I walked across the car park I saw someone laying on the concrete. It was the guard who had taken over from me and he was lying on his back clutching his rifle with the barrel resting on his shoulder and, if only he had been stood up, was in the correct position. He still had his hat on but otherwise was completely naked. It was a very hot night and I expected he would wake before dawn so I went back to bed and left him to sleep off the booze. He told me the next day he had not been seen by anyone else and had awakened the next man to take his place. We all had hangovers the next morning but the Aussie hospitality was great. We left with many thanks to our hosts and alot of "Good on yer Cobber" from them.

We got to our destination at a hutted camp about two miles from Kuala Lumpur in the afternoon. The camp was beside the river out in the country and some of the men I had worked with at K.L.

earlier in the year were there. I thought this could be a nice place to spend the rest of our time in the East but at this stage the thought of getting home seemed a long way away and most of us were determined to make the most of our time and enjoy ourselves as best we could.

I was anxious to see the town again and was not disappointed. It has some of the most beautiful buildings I have ever seen and more like a country town, with less poverty visible than in Singapore. We were to be here in Kuala Lumpur until a few days after the outbreak of the Japanese war. The climate seemed to be just as hot as Singapore but not so oppressive. The discipline also was more relaxed and easy going than being in Headquarters Far East at Fort Canning, Singapore.

After off-loading the Signal Office stores we had brought with us and having a very welcome shower, I was soon catching up with the gossip and rumours circulating since I was at K.L. last.

There was nothing to do within the camp, so if we went out we walked the two miles to the town and called in the Union Jack Club. Occasionally we finished up at the Eastern Hotel where there was dancing and a bar. Whisky was 50 cents a nip and beer 60 cents per half pint.

There were usually a few American business men staying in the hotel. We would go to the bar as near to them as possible and pool all our money which we arranged before hand which would amount to enough for one round of drinks. when we had drunk up someone would say "Ah well, thats it for tonight". Invariable the Americans would say "Come on you Guys, what are you drinking?" This would then leave us with enough money to buy a book of tickets off the dance girls. The tickets were 50 cents a book of ten tickets. Ten cents a dance! If there were more than five of us we used the outer cover of the book of tickets to push under the girls coffee cup. As the cover was the same colour as the tickets they seldom noticed and any way they did not always take a ticket for every dance.

The Americans usually asked questions about what it was like in the jungle. Each one of us tried to outdo the other about the horrors and dangers out there. The tigers, snakes, scorpions and ants which confronted us on manoeuvres. Not one of us had been more than a mile from the centre of Kuala Lumpur except on the main road .

Up until this time the only troops north of Singapore were British or Ghurkas. Soon some small units of Australian Engineers came up and were put in part of our camp. Shortly afterwards we moved from the Hutted East Camp to a large new building which had been built for housing married Coolies.

There was a balcony at the front and one square room about fifteen foot square and another narrow passage at the back and a space for a fire to cook the meals. This was more luxurious than anything we had since joining up. Two men to each room and an easily brushed floor with camp beds and a white sheet each. The Australians were in a hut not far away but used our mess room. This caused alot of trouble as the Australians got twice as much pay as we did. They also had their own cookhouse and were served up with twice as much food as us and even had jars of jam and marmalade. They sympathised with us and gave us some of their rations and let us dip into their jam jars! We complained daily to the Orderly Officer at every meal, and every day until told the next man to complain would be put on a charge for insubordination. The answer was to put a partition across the hut so that each could not see what the other was eating! They still used to throw bread over the partition for us.

After a week or so the British complained that we were doing all the Main Gate Guards and the Australians were off into town at four o'clock. Much to their disgust, they were ordered to mount guard every so often. The Guard always paraded for inspection on a parade ground which was overlooked by our Barrack Building.

The final straw that broke the Officers hearts and resulted in their asking for the Australians to be transferred to some other camp, was the night they were scheduled to mount the guard on the camp. The Barrack Block was three stories high and a balcony ran the whole length of each floor at the front. The Australians told us they had never been given any drill as they had been drafted into the Army just to be mechanics to service the trucks. They deliberately failed to tell the British Guard Commander this fact. Everyone who was not on guard duty clustered on the balconies, looking forward to a hilarious display of guard drill. We were not to be disappointed.

They wandered onto the parade ground and waited for the Sergeant. Some had shirt sleeves down and some sleeves rolled up. Half had shorts and the rest had longs. The Guard Commander bawled "Fall in" and they pushed and argued as to which row they should go in. A very crooked line eventually emerged but there were too many men in the back row. Every move was greeted by the watching men with a loud laugh. Eventually the Sergeant settled then in some sort of order of three ranks. The Orderly Officer arrived and they were given the "Open order for inspection". The drill is for the front row to take one step forward, the centre row to stand fast, and the back row to take one step back. The front row took a step back and the back row stayed put. Eventually the Sergeant got them in three ranks with space between them for the Orderly Officer to walk round for inspection. He failed to notice one man who did not even have a rifle. Next they were ordered to "Port Arms" so that the inside of the barrel could be examined. Finding the barrel almost blocked with dirt on the next mans rifle and the whole mechanism had not been oiled for a long time. The Officer asked him when he last cleaned his rifle. "I forget now but I think it was when we left Sydney." The same thing happened all through the ranks until he got to the middle of the centre row. This man did not have a rifle. "Where is your rifle?" asked the Officer, "Well Sir," he replied, "I was in a bar in Sydney the night before we left for Malaya and by the time I'd missed it I had forgotten where we had been, and I have never seen it since." The Officer was lost for words to say to the Australians. He told the Sergeant "Take this lot away and try and get them in some sort of order and I will see you on Inspection Rounds later tonight." He never turned up for the inspection and there was a notice on Company Orders that during Guard Mounting there will be nobody on the balconies of the Barrack Block.

We thanked the "Diggers" for their free show and the support in the canteen. They left the next day for another camp.

I had been suffering from a severe attack of Tinea on my feet. This was also known as Singapore Foot, or in England, Athletes Foot. I had not wanted to go sick as I might lose my place on the switchboard team. In the end it became almost unbearable. Army regulations made it compulsory to wear Army boots which were laced over the ankle and then woollen puttees wound round the top of the boots. This prevented the air getting to the feet and consequent sweating around the toes. The skin and flesh on the feet then started to peal off leaving open flesh wounds between the toes.

I went to the Medical Officer and was told to collect my Kit and go into hospital at Tanjong Malim. The "Hospital" was an old school building some twenty miles north of Kuala Lumpur. It was surrounded by Attap Huts built on wood platforms. The huts were illuminated by Hurricane lamps. What flush toilets there were, were not working and we had to use empty oil drums with a board across. Many of these were overflowing. The usual treatment of ointments and talcum powder proved to be quite useless and more drastic action was decided upon when the rot began to expose the bones in the toes. The whole of my feet up to the ankles were painted with a coating of Silver Nitrate which then set like a crust encasing the whole foot. Everything appeared to be alright and new skin formed and gradually the crust fell away until the last small area came away and the whole rot started all over again .

After this torture had been applied three times it appeared that the wounds were healed and I was given another week to get the new skin hardened off and get walking again.

The huts we were living in were wooden and had large open frames for light and air to come in. At night the paraffin Hurricane lamps were lit and hung onto the rafters. One evening shortly after darkness had descended more and more midges than usual came through the door and window spaces. Before long they were followed by a swarm of flying ants, apparently attracted to the light. They flew into the lamps and dropped on to the floor and others just flew in and alighted on the floor, the beds, and the patients. Soon every square inch of the area was covered with the discarded wings and bodies of these insects. Orderlies were called for and they swept them up with whisks and threw them through the door. However it was days before we got rid of all the bodies. They had got into the mattresses, our mess tins, sheets and kitbags. After about half an hour the swarm became a trickle and we began to sweep them up as fast as they came in.

Just abruptly as they started to come in the hut, the influx ceased and we were able to take our sheets out and shake them free of the ants and all the wings they had shed. It was mainly an Indian hospital and staffed by Indian Orderlies. Only the lower Caste could bring you drinking water and he was the guy that also took away your urine bottle. It was very complicated finding out who you asked to do any job for you.

The whole set up of the hospital was primitive. A few days later I was given my discharge and taken to Tanjong Malim Station and put on the train for Kuala Lumpur. I asked if I could wear gym shoes to travel in but the request was refused and I had to wear thick Army socks and laced up boots and then thick woollen puttees. This meant that no air was getting to my feet and after a two hour journey, when I got back to the barracks at Kuala Lumpur and took off my boots and socks, I could tell that the whole thing was starting all over again. The next morning on Sick Parade I was refused permission to go back on duty and told to avoid wearing any footwear except strapped sandals. It seemed so stupid to me taking great pains to cure me at the hospital they then make me put on boots knowing full well that these would reverse the cure.

During July and August we had had some Amber Alerts and twice were rounded up by the Military Police whilst off duty and in town and ordered to return to Barracks as fast as possible. This was in the early evening. The next morning we were told to pack our kit ready to move off if required. We paraded at midday but after about an hour we were stood down and resumed normal duties. However, orders went up, that all personnel when leaving the camp on or off duty must at all times carry rifles and ammunition. These must be at hand at all times when out of camp. We now realised that war was almost inevitable and only a matter of time.

Long discussions went on amongst the men. Where would the Japanese strike first? Singapore was considered well fortified with the big guns on the island covering the entrance to the Naval Base. The possibility of an attack on the main Malayan coast was also talked about. I do not remember the possibility of an attack via Thailand.

After my spell in hospital I was still on excused duties and not available for work. Some of the men had gone to Penang from our Office and they were short staffed. The Sergeant asked me if I would volunteer to go back on the usual shift on the switchboard. I was heartily sick of staying in Barracks all day and night and was very pleased to be asked to get back to work. I said "I will be only too glad to get back to work on one condition" "And what is it?" he asked. "Provided I can go on duty in my own sandals and not wear socks" I replied, expecting to get a rocket for even suggesting such outrageous dress could be accepted in the Signal Office. The Commanding Officer had to be consulted before he dare give me permission.

Much to my surprise and delight the ultimatum was accepted and I went back to work the next day. I was told not to come on parade but fall in after to get the truck to take us to the Office.

The speculation on the nearness of an attack from the Japanese was growing and the Signal Office became busier. Even at this late stage in our preparation the Signal Office at Kuala Lumpur was only connected to our Headquarters Far East at Singapore through the ordinary telephone exchanges.

We therefore had to rely on the Civilian Operators to put us through and we had no sort of priority. The only security was a scrambler phone which only the General Officer commanding and the Divisional Commanders were connected. It was procedure in the Signal Office that, when a new shift came on duty, they would check all calls being made through our exchange.

I was handing over one shift when the scrambler telephone was being used by General Percival and before I had time to tell the man relieving me that the scrambler was on the line, he cut in and said, "Bloody Chinese, they are talking on that line" and pulled the plug out! A good job we could blame the civilian exchange!

CHAPTER FOUR

WAR DECLARED

In the early afternoon of December 8th 1942 our shift had taken over the switchboard. Shortly afterwards, we were told to be ready to receive the code word "MATADOR" when all offices were to be contacted and told that hostilities against the Japanese Imperial Army had commenced. Some two hours later the code word came through and every line to every Office in the building had their indicator down and wanted a call. Every effort was being made to contact all Officers to report at Headquarters and there was a certain amount of near panic. Nevertheless, we were not caught totally unprepared, as we learned later, were the Americans at Pearl Harbour.

For the rest of our shift we were putting calls through as fast as we could. We had a sixty line switchboard and two of us to operate it. Obviously many calls were to H.Q. Far East at Singapore and the delay was around forty five minutes before we could get through to the civilian exchanges. This would not have been as bad if it had not been in Malaya, as radio contact was very unreliable and sometimes impossible. We had to use our own judgement as to which calls to give priority to and who to keep waiting, and we were the most unpopular section of the organisation at that time.

The relief shift came on at 1800 hours and we went back to camp. As we passed through the town everything seemed to be as usual and even we, could hardly believe that the forward troops were engaged in a battle on the Thailand border. We were greeted at the camp by the rest of the men wanting to know what was happening up country. There had been no air raid alerts and apart from the tightening of the guard, things were much as usual. We were 400 miles from the invasion of the Japanese which had taken place near the Thailand border. We were back on duty at the Signal Office at 2200 hours until 0600 hours the next morning.

The Signal Office had been "Blacked Out" with heavy black cloth which meant there was no fresh air entering the Office. We had large fans on the ceiling but these only tended to circulate the stale air down onto us and as the night wore on, the heat and the foul air became worse. There were three Operators on each shift, so we did get a break every so often from the actual operation of the switchboard. Motorcycle despatch riders were bringing in despatches from Penang and other Out Stations. Some of these reported being fired on by Snipers when passing through the jungle roads.

By now most of the Officers in charge of departments had been located and brought back from leave of from pleasure trips up country.

About one o'clock in the morning, I was speaking to H.Q. Singapore when there was a terrific bang and crunch. The operator at Singapore exclaimed "Hell! What was that?" and after a few seconds silence by him, but alot of background noise from the Office he said "Although we have had no warning sirens Japanese planes are bombing Singapore." That was the first shot of the war I had heard and was glad to be 400 miles away from it. We heard later that little damage was done and no more planes came over that night.

One instance of the difficulty of working with only two outside lines available to us was brought home to us during the night. One of the Officers at Kuala Lumpur wanted his opposite number at Singapore called, Lt. Jones. I rang Singapore and asked the exchange for Lt. Jones. Their Operator replied "Hold on please" and then "I am putting you through." A voice then came through to me saying "Kuala Lumpur, who do you wish to speak to?" I replied "Lt. Jones please." and then realised I was speaking to my partner on the K.L. exchange next to me. The point was the conversation was taking place via Singapore between two people sat side by side in Kuala Lumpur. Thus both our outside lines were being used for no purpose.

Complaints were coming through to our Officer that we were being very slow at getting calls for them. We decided on a priority code for all calls. This was, first General Percival, then Scrambler Phone to H.Q. Far East, followed by Deputy Director Medical Services and then whoever was polite and grateful and lastly, anyone who had put in a complaint. That was the end of the complaints.

We kept telling all the Officers we were in touch with, how vital it was to get a direct line to Singapore. It appeared that the Telegraph company refused to let us have one and said they needed all the lines they had for civilian use. However, it appeared General Percival insisted and they reluctantly allowed us one direct line for our sole use to Headquarters Far East at Fort Canning.

The following day a man came to dig a trench and the holes to put the telegraph poles in. Whilst I was getting some fresh air during a period off the switchboard I got into conversation with him. He was a smallish elderly Malay and spoke very good English. I remarked on this and he said he had worked in England and France and Russia and Germany. I was very doubtful about this until he said, "I travel all over the world when a small boy. I visit all European capitals and Australia." I asked him what he did to get to all these places. He said, "Many years ago I was the Black Boy assistant to a Magician called Houdini and he took me with him on all his travels." I asked him if he got a lot of money for his job. "No" he said, "I was only paid five shillings a week, and Houdini paid my board and lodgings." Fame had sure passed him by. The following day he brought us his well thumbed passport, and one entry was signed by the then Prime Minister of Australia especially allowing him to enter Australia.

By this time, rumours were rife that we had defeated the Japanese landings. These were followed by less optimistic reports that our forces were holding a line on the border with Thailand. Kuala Lumpur affairs went on as if nothing had happened and nobody took the war very seriously. A blackout of sorts was in operation, but as the shops only have shutters and no windows, it was very difficult to prevent some light showing.

The whole civilian organisation was anti Army and would not co-operate with anything the Army wanted. I recall a telephone conversation between the Deputy Director Medical Services and the Controller of Railways. The D.D.M.S. wanted to get a train load of wounded men from the front, who were at Alor Star, through to hospital in Singapore. The railwayman said "No, it is impossible, the Red Cross train will have to wait until the midnight passenger train has left Penangs there are a lot of high ranking civilians on board that train. Therefore it cannot make way for your Red Cross train." For two days the Controller of the Railways refused point blank to give the wounded troops any priority over the scheduled passenger trains. Consequently, they were shunted into sidings to allow other trains to pass them so that there was no interference of passenger train schedules!

Two days after the war started I was asked on the telephone by the commanding Officer of the Anti-Aircraft Units in Singapore if I could put him in touch with the R.A.F. Officer at their Headquarters who was responsible for Recognition Signals for Ground to Air Communications. To save time I telephoned the R.A.F. and asked for the Officer Commanding the R.A.F. who I could put the Anti-Aircraft people in touch with. No-one could give me the information I wanted but eventually I pointed out the information was vital to prevent the shooting down of our own aircraft by our guns. Someone at the R.A.F. eventually promised he would get an Officer to give the required information to the Anti-Aircraft Gunners. Sadly, in the meantime, two of our planes were shot at by our own guns. The Signal Office was now part of the War Machine and what we did, and how quickly we did it was of vital importance for all communications.

One evening, when I happened to be alone on the switchboard at Kuala Lumpur shortly after the outbreak of hostilities, someone in the Intelligence Office, who seemed very agitated, asked for a Kuala Lumpur number. In monitoring the call I learned that the Intelligence Officer had run into a cyclist and left him lying injured at the side of the road, and he asked his wife to call for an Ambulance but avoid revealing who she was, or for whom she was speaking. As soon as the conversation was over I received a call, which must have been from the Main Post and Telegraph Exchange, asking me for the telephone number of the caller and who he was speaking to. One of the remarks in the earlier conversation was asking if the victim of the accident was a native and, when the answer was yes, one of the callers said "Oh well, that is not so bad." As the Operators were mostly Eurasians I pulled out the cord and broke the call down. The last thing I needed was anything that could upset race relations or relations between the Army and the civilians .

In those days, the race and anti-race relations industry had not been invented and we never had any problems with the Chinese, Japanese, Malays, Indians or any other race. If there were any fights, they were usually between the British and the Australians! Those were usually good natured "belt-ups". As British soldiers, the only race we were not popular with was the British White Colonials. Their attitude changed dramatically when the Japanese invaded.

If we were their guests on their own ground we were made welcome and royally entertained. It seemed to be a status symbol to have to dislike the Army. This was highlighted when the railways refused to give us priority even in wartime.

Christmas Day, 1941, was marked by what could have been a difficult situation. The shift I was on went on duty at six o'clock in the morning and was due to be relieved at one o'clock. We were promised some sort of Christmas Dinner and two bottles of beer when we came off duty at one. One o'clock came and passed, and two o'clock passed and no sign of our relief shift arriving at the Signal Office. They arrived at 2.30 in a merry mood, but we were in no state to welcome them. Tempers were high, but no blows were struck. We embarked and drive back to our Billet looking forward to a better than usual Christmas Dinner. After getting our eating utensils we arrived at the Mess Room and found all the tables were littered with dirty plates and empty beer bottles but no places reserved for us. We marched into the kitchen and asked the Cook where was our dinner. "There is nothing left" he said, "Nobody told us about a late shift coming in." He showed us the boiler with the remains of a stew in it but nothing could be found but water. We marched in a body to the Sergeant Majors tent and he came out to us but all he could say was "If there is none left, you cannot have any dinner." We demanded to see an Officer. He stood firm and tried to stop us going to the Officers quarters. He was obviously very drunk and as he stumbled we pushed and he went headlong into the drain ditch. The Officers heard the row and came dashing out to see what the noise was about. We needed to get some satisfaction before the Sergeant recovered and got out of the ditch. The outcome was the cooks were brought in and a fresh meal was served but there was no beer left. Fortunately, the Officer was sympathetic and the incident was forgotten.

By this time the Japanese had begun to push our front line back and the retreat from the Thai border was serious. Some of our Forward Signal Groups were now coming back to Kuala Lumpur. After the fall of Ipoh, some of our men had acquired large quantities of cigarettes still in their wooden cases. Also some bottles of beer, whisky, gin and other spirits. These came from a bombed department store in Ipoh from which everyone had fled down to Singapore.

After the canteen closed for the night back at camp we held parties in our rooms. The men who had the drink brought it round to the rooms and we filled the fire buckets with cold water and put them in the middle of the floor filled with Champagne bottles! These parties went on until the early hours of the morning. The Barrack Block echoed to the cries of "Come around to my place." Eventually, the complaints were heeded and everyone retired leaving large quantities of half smoked cigarettes and loads of empty bottles. All this had to be disposed of before parade as the bottles were obviously looted.

Somehow the Commanding Officer found out that there was a load of contraband in the trucks which had come down from Penang. The order was issued that all alcohol and cigarettes which had been obtained illegitimately had to be handed in to the Quartermasters Stores by six o'clock that evening or all concerned would be on serious charges. Frantic efforts were made to salvage the cigarettes and two wooden cases were put through a skylight and into a space between the ceiling and the flat roof of the Barrack Block.

All manner of hiding places were used for the contraband, and men were to be seen wandering around with bulging shirt fronts and sneaking a place to hide the loot. When the time came for the contraband to be handed in, drivers of the trucks took along a bottle or two of beer and whisky and a few packets of cigarettes explaining that, after a very meticulous search of their vehicles, they had found this stuff but of course they had no idea how it had got into their wagons. During these parties, there were few complaints from the more sober residents of the Barracks and when we were eventually ordered back to our own quarters around 4 o'clock there had been no fights, no damage to property, and no blood spilt. We just had four hours of make-believe fun in a childish way. Reality would not be long before it caught up with us.

News of the fighting up country was always alarming as each day the retreat of our front line troops was bringing the time nearer when we would be pushed back from Kuala Lumpur towards Singapore. Our despatch riders were coming in from forward areas and reporting being fired on by snipers from the jungle and the rubber plantations. Rumours of the use of Gas in the fighting was also rife, but never proven .

A new Officer Commanding Signals, who had only recently arrived in Malaya, was put in charge of us in Kuala Lumpur. The men who were working the Signal Office were now experienced in operating under war conditions. Discipline may have been a little relaxed but efficiency was maintained and we all knew each other and got on well together. Under the circumstances we were a happy lot. This seemed to irritate the new Officer and all sorts of petty restrictions and inspections were initiated by him. Those of us who were on Signal Office duty in shifts were ordered to attend all parades except when actually on duty. This meant we came off duty at 6 a.m. after being working from ten the previous night and we then had to get into battle dress order and parade at seven. We did not get breakfast before nine and only had three hours sleep before going back on duty at two o'clock.

Before the Japanese war started we had been on a nightime exercise in the jungle. When the ammunition and stores were checked on our return a shortage of four rounds of ammunition was reported. A preliminary enquiry had been held and adjourned to a later date and when the war started everyone thought that would be the end of the affair as bullets were being used by the thousand up country. Not with this guy. The charges were to be heard at Ipoh which is north of Kuala Lumpur. Witnesses for the prosecution and for the defence were detailed to appear at a date fourteen days hence. Military Police were also involved and all was set for a trial about the loss of four rounds of ammunition. Much to the chagrin of the Commanding Officer before the due date, Ipoh had fallen into enemy hands and the whole episode was forgotten .

Orders went up that the present Signal Office Personnel would be replaced by the recent intake of men belonging to the unit which the Commanding Officer belonged. Those who had been on the shifts were told to parade and we were all given various fatigues about the camp such as cleaning the latrines, digging out drains and sweeping the parade ground. About midday the shift I had been on was rounded up hurriedly and told to be at the transport point in ten minutes. We duly turned up at the Signal Office and found a situation of almost panic. All the lights on the sixty line switchboard were lit and waiting to be put through and the only direct line to Singapore was not being used. A call from General Percival to be put through on the Scrambler Phone to H.Q. Far East Asia Command had been kept waiting as the new man did not know how to initiate such a call.

Despatch riders had been given telegrams which were not on their run and others were allowed to leave without routine post. Within half an hour we had sorted out the mess, but alot of damage had been done to urgent operations. The next shift was ordered to bring some of the old shift with them to help instruct in the workings of a Signal Office .

The next company orders detailed all Officers, Non-Commissioned Officers and the whole of the Camp Personnel not on duty to parade in full battle order with rifles and all our kit at 1900 hours on the Main Parade Ground. Each section was told to parade at the side of the transport allocated to them and all trucks were to face north on one side of the parade ground. We stood to attention and the Commanding Officer came round with an Officer holding a torch. This was shone at our boots to check for shine and to our equipment to see that it was properly packed and all straps fastened.

The time came, around nine in the evening, when usually the Japanese planes came over on their way to bomb Singapore. The order was given to start up all vehicles and as the Commander came to each truck, to switch on the headlights on to full beam. By the time the inspection was finished all the men were convinced we had a traitor in our midst and he was giving the Japs a fully illuminated target at which to aim. All confidence in this man was now gone and all orders we were given from him were suspect. With all the engines running we could not have heard the planes if they had come over. The Japanese forces were now only three days away from Kuala Lumpur at their present rate of progress. We would be moving back any day now. The order came next day for every one to pack all their kit ready to move.

CHAPTER FIVE

THE RETREAT FROM KUALA LUMPUR

Our shift took over from the night shift at seven a.m. We had all our kit with us including a few souvenirs to take home! The whole Signal Office was in turmoil. All the various branches were packing and no-one knew where they would be tomorrow. All those Signals Personnel who were not on the Duty Shift would be leaving straight from the Barracks to establish a Communications Centre further south.

We, as Switchboard Operators, had to be the last to leave in case anyone needed to telephone at the last moment. However, all our equipment and stores were loaded and still some units were using the exchange. I had a feeling of what was going to happen as the Sergeant had been particularly pleasant to me and asked after my welfare during the morning. I was right. The order was given for all except Switchboard Operators to board their transport. That left three of us and the Sergeant. He came over to me and said "You will stay behind until there are no calls left on the switchboard, and here is an axe. You will destroy any equipment left including the switchboard and all its connections. You will sever all cables leading into the offices and all possible fixed equipment. Your Commanding Officer will then pick you up and bring you to join the rest of the Unit."

I watched all the trucks leaving and as the noise died away the noise of the birds and insects seemed louder than I had ever heard before. I knew the usual excuse for picking me to stay behind would be I was childless. Or more it seemed to me, sometime, I would hardly be missed! "

The switchboard buzzed and a light came on. I answered expecting someone to ask if it was true we had abandoned Kuala Lumpur. A male voice very calmly asked if that was Army Headquarters and then he said, "If you want to call here, I am leaving now and there is an almost new motor cycle you can have." I said "Thank you. I may need some transport before long." He gave me the address and we wished each other well. At least, I thought, if my Officer fails to turn up I will have the means to get the hell out of here. I had the further offer of a car that was being abandoned as the owners fled south. After a couple of hours the Officer appeared and we set to with the axe and chopped viciously until all the switchboards entrails spewed out from the frame. I seemed to get an element of satisfaction out of destroying this thing that had caused us so much worry.

This was my first taste of retreat and I did not like it. As we drove through the town on our way south the atmosphere of despair and bewilderment seemed to have left a strange sort of hush over the area. All traffic seemed to be going Singapore way. My Officer was not very informative as to where we were going. Arriving at some huts we appeared to have moved back some thirty miles and set up a Telephone Exchange in a disused rubber plantation office. After a couple of uneventful days we were ordered to retreat further down the main Singapore road in convoy .

We were short of transport and our Corporal went into the village and commandeered a "Piggy Bus". These were small sixteen seater buses which plied to villages and outlying parts of towns. Normally they would be carrying twenty or thirty people, some baskets of chickens and perhaps a few baskets with small pigs in them. Fortunately, he found one which was not very full and exchanged it for a bit of paper telling the driver he would be compensated later by the War Office. The Corporal had been in charge of a truck and had come down from Penang but his truck was given to another driver. The load that he had brought down country on the other truck was in a pile at the side of the road. There were four of us to go with him. We went to help him load up what, from the outside looked to be telephones, radio sets, telephone lines on drums and the usual Signals equipment. From the centre of the pile came a large His Masters Voice Radio Gramaphone in a polished walnut cabinet with a cupboard which was well stocked with records of recent times. This was hurriedly and furtively loaded into a recess at the back of the bus and quickly hidden by legitimate Signals material. This was followed by a carton of six bottles of whisky and a further carton of gin. Next was a carton of Nestles condensed milk and a wooden crate of cigarettes. We were fortunate enough to be at the rear of the convoy. We travelled along drinking whisky with condensed milk and listening to the latest records.

The gramaphone was fortunately a wind-up one. Passing various bus stops we were assailed by would be fare paying passengers, but thought it prudent not to stop.

The convoy turned into a clearing in a rubber plantation and two of us went to try and find a decent place to spend the night. We spotted a newly built hut which was on stilts but obviously deserted. We got the bus as near as we could and took all our kit up the stairs and thought we had got away from the rest of the party. We were surprised when our Sergeant found us and we had to go and stay in the bus for the night. The comfortable house was taken over by the Sergeants.

The next day I was offered the choice of manning an Anti-Aircraft Gun or cooking for the Sergeants Mess. I took one look at the gun which was a shallow trench in the middle of a sandy clearing, and decided on the Sergeants mess. I had lived on whisky and condensed milk for the past 24 hours and the idea of having access to the Sergeants Mess appealed to me.

When I reported to the Mess I was given three small tins of sausages. I divided the sausages equally and had two left over so I decided I didn't want any argument among the Sergeants and I ate the two spare ones before they appeared. I was also able to have a decent cup of tea with lots of sugar but no milk.

The next stop was at Serambam where there was a Post Telegraph Exchange manned by civilians. Three Signals men including myself were detailed to go into the Telephone Exchange and monitor the civilian operators. We were provided with revolvers but as most of the conversations were in Chinese, Malay or Urdu, we could only act as a deterrent. We stayed there for a couple of days before we were again on the retreat towards Singapore.

The old bus had a puncture in the rear tyre and the last few miles were covered on the rim. Whilst the Corporal went into the town to commandeer another vehicle we off-loaded the bus and stacked all the luggage in a heap trying to keep the loot out of sight. It was not long before he was back with a flat wagon which was all of fifteen years old. As we were finishing re-loading our new transport, the Commanding Officer came up and saw the cartons and gramaphone already on the lorry. The Corporal said they were in the bus when he picked it up! The Officer insisted we dump the gramaphone and the whisky and gin. This was off-loaded at the opposite side of the wagon and we proceeded to load all the Signal Office crates and boxes at one side of the truck and when the load got high enough to hide us, two men went to the other side and loaded the contraband. We had a tarpaulin and very quickly covered the whole load ready for leaving the following morning.

The first time the convoy stopped our truck nearly ran into the one ahead. The brakes were almost non-existent. When we started up again we were told to go on ahead and the rest of the convoy would catch us up before nightfall. We had gone some ten miles when enemy aircraft we spotted heading to cross our road. We were going downhill and the truck was not stopping very quickly so the driver said "Jump off and I'll run it onto the verge of the road". He had a bumpy ride but it came to a stop safely. We took cover in the bush and the planes ignored us.

One of the men with us was a cook and we were carrying some of his knives etc. We stopped occasionally and had a swig or two of the whisky laced with condensed milk and by early afternoon we were getting merry and careless.

I was riding on the truck stood behind the drivers cab when he said that the warning lights were not working. I said I would hand signal if he would tell me when he was going to turn. The cook said nobody but the driver must signal. I told him "The driver cannot signal for a left turn". I still did the hand signals when the driver asked me. This upset the cook and we had an argument. The outcome was that he drew a butchers knife out from amongst the stuff on the truck and said "Next time you bloody Signal, I'll cut you bloody throat!" One of the other men on the platform who had been keeping a look out for any trouble from the Jap snipers or bombers came to my assistance and we managed to take the knife off him and roll him up in a blanket. The condensed milk and whisky diet had not been good for him and he went to sleep so we covered him up under the tarpaulin sheet.

The driver had heard the commotion and stopped to see what the trouble was. We told him of the threat and how we had wrestled with him amongst the load. He had fallen and hit his head against a wooden crate and we had put the knife out of reach. We resumed our journey, but I kept a very close watch on where he was lying as if he recovered he would have me for supper.

The Sergeant came over to see us as we drew up on the grass verge to bring the truck to a stop. He called out our names and we all answered until he called "Slater" and there was no answer. We had forgotten about the cook whose name was Slater. "Oh yes" I said "he is under the tarpaulin on the side of the truck." One of us untied the ropes and two took the pegs out of the sideboard and Slater rolled off the platform and down into the undergrowth, still wrapped in his blanket. We told the Sergeant he had been unwell and thought he should see the Medical Officer. A stretcher was called for and he was taken away before he woke up from his stupor. He appeared on parade the next morning and no-one asked any questions, and he never said anything about the episode of the day before. A cooking job was found for him and I never saw him again. For this I was thankful as he did have a nasty temper coupled with a nasty knife.

We'd had very little food or drink over the last three days apart from the whisky and milk, and anyway we had lost the taste for the whisky/milk cocktail. I was wishing we had found a spare tyre for the old Piggy Bus instead of getting the flat wagon to replace it. When we abandoned the old bus in order to deny it to the Japs, the engine was started on the edge of a ravine, the accelerator was jammed down with a board and the brake released and away she went over the bonnet to the bottom of the ravine.

The next day we retreated further towards Singapore and slept in some huts which had been abandoned by the Australians, very hurriedly, a couple of days before. We did manage to get a supper there and breakfast the next morning. The Officers did a reconnoitre of the camp and found a large hole in the ground with a telephone switchboard in and that it connected with an Australian camp and also to the camp which was where the Signals intended to setup a Signal Office. There were other connections on the Board but none were answering. The hole was covered by a round tent but no other protection. Another switchboard operator and myself were detailed to man the post. We took it in turns and were able to get some food. The Sergeant came round and said the rest of the unit was leaving for another camp and I was to stay there until 6.00 p.m. when he would send some transport for me .

The whole exercise was useless. I was alone with three lines going to different places, but none of the connections were of any help to anybody. After what seemed a long time, I had no calls, I rang my Signal Office and asked the time. It was three o'clock. I suggested that as there were no calls coming through could they not pick me up earlier than six. The message came back "You have to stay until the time given to you before, that is 6.00 p.m."

Everything was so quiet and the atmosphere down below was hot and stuffy. I decided to surface and have a look round the camp and see if I could find anything to eat or drink. I found a large Mess tent with three rows of tables, forms even table cloths. Scattered over the tables were pieces of bread, lumps of cheese, pots of jam, mugs of tea and empty fish tins. All this food was open to the air and flies covered most of it. There was nothing I dare eat as it appeared to have been abandoned very hurriedly probably three days before. There were even one or two photographs and other personal belongings which would not have been left if they had not been in a hurry. I wandered all round the camp area but found nothing worth picking up.

I noticed that there were telegraph poles with wires leading into the dugout switchboard, four in all. I looked up to see where the wires led to and suddenly noticed a V formation of planes heading directly towards me. I did not have to wait until they came nearer to know whose they were. We had not seen a British plane for days and learned afterwards that they had all left for Java a few days before. I kept them insight from the dugout steps and hoped they would pass over on their way to Singapore. I saw the bomb doors open as they were coming towards me and reckoned that the camp I was in looked like their target for a few bombs. From where I was it seemed as if they had dropped the lot.

After about a minute everything went quiet and I could hear the planes going away from me. I emerged soon after the last bomb fell wondering what damage had been done around the camp. The main damage appeared to be the overhead lines and following from my dugout I realised that I was probably totally cut off from all outside telephones.

None of the huts were damaged, but there was a direct hit on the Medical Orderly's tent and hundreds of contraceptives were scattered all around the area. The other craters were just around the camp and had done little damage. I went back below and tested all the lines, they were all dead except the one to the Signals Office.

I rang through to the Office and spoke to someone I thought was the switchboard operator. "Would you tell the C.O. that all the lines here are down except the one I am speaking to you on, and there seems no point in my staying here any longer." A very abrupt message was given. " This is the Brigadier speaking. What time were you told to leave there?" "Eighteen hundred hours Sir" I replied. "Well you will stay there until eighteen hundred hours then." was the very curt reply and the telephone was slammed down.

I had no idea where I was and had an hour or more to wait to see if anyone would come and pick me up. Eventually, at dusk, my friend with the Packhard arrived. I was very pleased to see him and glad he had arrived before the Japanese. I asked him where we were going and apparently he had no further instructions, so we decided to head down the main road to Singapore. It was a brilliant moonlit night so we had no need to use car headlights. We crossed the Causeway between Johore Bahru and Singapore without incident.

We managed to scrounge something to eat at the first place we found where there were Army troops. They told us there were some Signals troops further down the road. We arrived to join them, but they had no spare space in their tents so we were glad of the big car to sleep in. It was some protection against the mosquitos.

The next morning I was detailed to join a special unit to set up and operate a scrambler phone in the bush. We had a small Army truck and loaded it up with the necessary cables, telephones and quite heavy instruments which did the scrambling and unscrambling of conversations. The purpose of the exercise was to set this up in the bush within sight of the Johore Causeway and to keep in touch with the general organising of the evacuation of all troops from Malaya to Singapore over the only escape route by road that there was. We had to link in with the main cable following the road and setup the instruments somewhere where the trees would give us best cover. This meant dragging the equipment some distance through thick scrub. There were only three Signals men on this party and we were told to keep in touch with evacuation units the other side of the bridge and General Percival and his entourage would arrive at about midnight.

As soon as all the units and transport who would be able to get across, before we blew the bridge over the Causeway. The signal to detonate the charges under the bridge would be given by General Percival from the scrambler phone. We watched the engineers laying the explosives under the bridge arches. We had a good view of the length of the Causeway. The mosquitos were biting and the heat was stifling. We dare not smoke as the undergrowth was tinder dry.

Just before midnight on February 8th 1942 what remained of the Scottish Regiments crossed the bridge led by the Pipers of the Argyll and Sutherland Highlanders playing Scottish airs. They were followed by all those troops who had not been able to make the rendezvous in Johore. Some were on foot and others in cars, troop carriers and all kinds of vehicles. We could see all this and were praying that the Japanese would not strike on the ground or from the air. The evacuation was at first a torrent of men and machines, but gradually it thinned out and we could only discern a few stragglers. An Ambulance arrived on the road and stopped at the nearest point to our hideout.

A wondered what a Red Cross Ambulance was coming to us for. To my horror out of it climbed the three top ranking Officers of the Army. I felt absolutely disgusted that they had come over the Causeway in the Red Cross Ambulance when they were on a wholly military mission .

We immediately made contact through the scrambler phone with the Bridgehead Office on the Johore side of the Causeway. We remained in contact with them for about an hour. The motor traffic over the bridge ceased and apart from a few stragglers on bicycles or even on foot, the evacuation seemed to be over. The engineers who were nearer to the bridge were given the signal to demolish some of the arches. There was a terrific explosion and a great cloud of debris went high into the air.

The last escape route from Johore to Singapore by road was destroyed. Regrettably the damage had not been as great as we had hoped for and it was not long before the Japanese had it re-opened.

The object of our mission was accomplished. The three Generals returned to their Red Cross Ambulances and drove away into the night. I hope they realised how annoyed we were at them misusing an ambulance marked with the Red Cross.

We dismantled the scramble phone and cut the cables and loaded them onto our truck and drove back to our camp. The Causeway at Johore was the only bridge link between Malaya and the island of Singapore. It was now February 8th 1942. The whole campaign to date had only lasted seven weeks and we had been on the retreat almost the whole of the time .

I could not expect anything other than surrender eventually as we had no, repeat no, air support of any sort. The Japanese bombers came over in formations of 27 planes at a time and the only opposition was a small amount of anti-aircraft fire.

The total lack of opposition by the Japanese to our evacuation of the mainland was unbelievable. Not a plane came over and although the enemy was within shelling distance, no shots were fired. We drove along the main road to Singapore town without lights as the moonlight was sufficient for us to see clearly. We passed a camp which seemed to be very active and there was a smell of cooking, so we stopped and begged a meal from them. We risked a couple of hours sleep in the car drawn into a rubber plantation. We spent the day touring round to see if we could find anyone of our own unit. We eventually found a unit of Signals who appeared to have cooking facilities and a few trucks and tents. The site was on a hillside and next to a cemetery where long rows of graves had been dug to bury the dead from the bombing of Singapore .

The sun was setting and I remember how, as it went down beyond the horizon, an enormous V was formed by the suns rays. I was just getting a cigarette from a packet of "Victory V" free issue Army cigarettes. I thought could this be a good omen for us. It was not to be .

This was not a proper camp, but they had a Field Kitchen and that was a great attraction as I'd had only a few meals over the last four days. We all compared notes as to where we had been and what we had seen and heard. Put all our conversations together and the story was grim indeed. There was grass growing around the cemetery borders and I decided that would be softer than sleeping on a gravestone. I put down by ground sheet, wrapped myself in a blanket and promptly fell asleep. The night was uneventful except for a few tracer shells lighting up the area.

Most of the men were Signals so I joined them for breakfast and went to their camp base which was a large tent beside a river. I was able to get a shower, general clean up and shave. Their Sergeant allotted me a bed for the following night. This meant I had somewhere to leave my kit bag in which I had a camera, photographs and a few personal possessions.

I joined the rest of the men on parade in the morning. A call was made for a switchboard operator and I was given the job. I was presented to an Officer and he told me where to go and operate a small Signal Office situated just outside the Naval Base.

I was getting ready to leave when bullets started to rip through the canvas and embedded themselves in the tent pole and others thudded into the beds. Some of us who had our rifles handy rushed outside but could not find where the shots had come from. Probably from the trees on the opposite side of the river. There was nothing much we could do as if they were snipers they would have been away quickly.

My orders were to report back to the camp that evening so I just took my large ruck sack and blanket and left my other gear in my bed space to come back to in the evening. The Signal Office we had been sent to was in a wooded area with a perimeter fence of attap panels. It was just an attap hut with five divisions in and the switchboard was in the middle section at the far side of the office. I was told that the actual switchboard we were operating was one that had been taken from the Queen Mary before She was converted to a Troopship. It was rather luxurious for Army Signals!

There were two other operators working but after explaining who the lines were connected to, they both drifted away and left me alone with the Exchange. A Signals Officer came into the hut and I asked him where the other operators had gone. He was not very interested and ordered me to stay at the Board until a relief came. An hour or so later I realised I appeared to be the only bloke around this place, and as I could not raise anyone on the lines of the Board, I decided to take a look round. The place was deserted. The man that was supposed to be with me had disappeared and so had everybody else.

The Japanese had mounted a gun somewhere near the Causeway and it was intermittently firing into Singapore town. I could also hear mortar fire not far away. I had no transport and all I could do was wait .

Eventually a despatch rider arrived and said he would stick around for a while and if no-one turned up he would give me a lift back to Singapore. A Staff Car drew up at the gate and one of our Brigadiers came into the Office with his Batman. I explained by problem. He said "Well I will take you back to Singapore." "Yes Sir, thank you Sir" I replied with alacrity. "Should we destroy the switchboard and equipment Sir?" He agreed and sent his Batman to find some petrol. He returned with a four gallon tin of what I thought was paraffin and I emptied it over everything in the Office and stepped outside. I threw a match in through the entrance. Whoof!! the fumes exploded and everything seemed to alight at once and the whole row of rooms burst into flames. Some of the trees caught fire and shot flames and smoke into the sky.

We all retreated rapidly to the Sentry Hut at the main entrance to the site. A Lieutenant Signals arrived and joined us in the hut. We made a formidable war force of one Brigadier, one Lieutenant Signals, one Batman and one Signalman holed up in a small Sentry Box in charge of a burning Signal Office.

We heard the noise of an aircraft, and then the whistle of a bomb falling. It landed some hundred yards away, but we all fell to the floor. The Brigadier had only one arm and lost his balance. We were uninjured. He told us the road back to my camp had been overrun by the Japanese and we were to find our way back as best we could. I thought it would be safer to go with the Lieutenant in his car than ride in the Brigadiers Staff Car.

I got into the Morris Eight car and the driver suggested we open the sun roof and I stand on the seat and carry my Rifle at the ready with my head stuck out through the roof. We left the Brigadier and his Batman to make their own way back to Singapore. We had to pass along side the Golf Course and their were half a dozen bloated dead cows lying around with all four legs stuck up in the air. As we were rounding a bend in the road and old truck passed us on the Golf Course itself. That really was cutting corners. The truck was piled high with all the owners possessions and a number of people were clinging on desperately to get away from the battle as quickly as possible .

As we got further along the road a number of our Infantry men deployed themselves across the Golf Course in bunkers and behind bushes. We joined them and my Officer said we would stay with these men. We took up position lying in the grass. This was to be my first battle under rifle fire. We could see figures in the distance coming over the horizon and spreading over the course. They were confirmed by the man with the field glasses as enemy troops. The Officer I was with suddenly decided that his car, which was just off the road, was an invitation to the enemy and a danger to the troops. I think the nearness of the Japanese had an influence of his decision to leave the area.

The Infantry men confirmed that there was now only one road back to Singapore that was not taken by the enemy. This was the Bukit Timah road. We decided to try that one. I remounted the wee Morris and took up my stance. Our outfit was the nearest thing to a tank that was available. The only tank we had originally had got bogged down and been abandoned the first day of the war.

We took the road suggested by the Troops and hoped we would not encounter the enemy just around the corner of the road. We were fired on by snipers, but I could not see from where the shots were coming. After another four or five miles we were again fired on, but we safely passed through. Just around a bend in the road we came upon an Australian Unit who were parked and had fires going to cook some food .

We exchanged information and told them of the firing which we had encountered quarter of a mile away. They appeared quite unconcerned and said they had been fired on once or twice whilst being where they were. As we got nearer to Singapore town a Japanese plane came over and dropped pamphlets. These told us to surrender and suggested that the Americans were up to no good with our women folk back in England .

At the time, we were passing the Ford factory, where, later the cease-fire was to be signed .

I was left at the Engineers Building in Singapore town centre by the Officer who had given me a lift from the Naval Base Signal Office. I joined a motley crew of various regiments but mostly Royal

Signals. This was a four storey building and a protective wall had been built around the four sides of the area and sandbags were placed at each entrance. There was a make shift cookhouse on the ground floor.

I spent the first night trying to sleep o the top floor but about eleven o'clock the bombers came over and dropped some bombs but missed us entirely and there was also some shelling from the heavy gun based in Johore. Things quietened down at about 4 a.m. and I did get some sleep only to dream that I was about to roll off the edge of the building after a bomb had demolished the outer wall.

The next day we just hung around and were told we could go up to the mess on the top of the hill at Fort Canning. Shortly after leaving to go for a midday meal the long range gun opened up, and as we looked up towards the Fort, a shell went straight into a garage beside a house on the hillside and blew it to pieces along with the car. There were four of us who had gone up together. The Other Ranks Mess was in Fort Canning itself. We just arrived at the door when a lone plane came over and dropped a bomb in the courtyard. There were a few injuries as we had no warning to go to the shelters. We managed to finish our meal and then the sirens went for all those not on duty to go to the shelter. There was a young Indian lad who said he had lost his nerve and had been in the shelter for the last twelve hours. We we surfaced we found two men had been injured by shrapnel in the raid, but little material damage had occurred.

Fort Canning itself was of course the prime target now for both the long range gun and the bombers. We decided we would get back down the hill as fast as possible as the Japanese gunners had the range of the Fort. As we walked down the hill, we heard the whistle of another shell coming from Johore Battery. We took cover behind a building and waited for the bang. The shell landed lower down the hill and made a large hole in the ground but did little damage. We had gone some two hundred yards, when the dreaded whistle was heard again. We sheltered in the porch of a Chapel and the shell hit the building we had just left and raised it to the ground. As it was usual for this gun to fire five rounds and then cease for fifteen minutes we reckoned we could make the next shelter before the next round. Sure enough the whistle was heard and we took cover. From where we were we could see the Chapel which we had just left. The shell went straight into the side of the building, the edifice trembled and then there was an enormous explosion and fire and minor explosions as the whole building fell apart.

It appeared to have been full of ammunition. We managed to get back to our Billet without further adventure.

As soon as darkness fell the shelling increased and three of us decided to go onto the roof of the building. In those days this was about the tallest building in the area. We had a fantastic view fo the whole town and fires were burning all around. Shells were coming over thick and fast and starting more fires. The noise of explosions and the crack of the guns firing, now not very far away, and the thuds as a formation aircraft dropped its bombs all around us was deafening.

I decided to sleep on a landing of the stairs, as they were in the middle of the building and less vulnerable from a near miss. We were given some corned beef on a slice of bread and some tea for breakfast. We had nothing to do and no-one seemed to make any use of us and we were getting more and more apprehensive as to what would happen when we were taken prisoner by the Japanese.

There was an open Ford V8 truck going up to Fort Canning so we hitched a lift to go for some food. We had only gone a hundred yards when the Japs opened fire with mortars. We screeched to a stop and jumped out and dropped down into the open sewers which lined all the streets of the town. These were some four feet deep and a yard wide and so we could get our heads below the road level and watch the mortar bombs bursting a few feet away. The big gun from Johore was also in action and when the usual five rounds had been fired we got back on the truck which was untouched. We had not gone far when the mortar attack was resumed and as the explosions were both infront and behind us, the driver put on speed. I was stood up on the lorry and looking over the cab, (we had an open topped wagon) when a shell burst about twenty yards ahead but another landed some ten yards infront of us and there was no way the driver could stop. It failed to explode and as we went towards it, it was spinning round .

I held my breath and was sure it would explode beneath us. I turned and looked back and, glory be, the thing was still spinning round and had failed to detonate. After a few more near misses we arrived at Fort Canning, but again we had to go to the shelter. Obviously the Japs were now surrounding us on three sides and the fourth side was the sea, so there was no prospect of leaving the island. The last ship had left with women and children and some Australians two days before.

Back at the Engineers Building, I was feeling depressed and a little afraid. When we were outside dodging the bombs we had no time to be afraid. Survival was more important.

I was at the entrance to the building behind the sandbags when two men in civilian clothes ran across the road and wanted volunteers to try and rescue some Red Cross stores from a building that was on fire not far away. Three of us rushed back with them and found that one end of the warehouse was burning but we got in the other end. It was stacked high with bales of field dressings and bandages, cartons of pills and medicines and I presume all sorts of medical equipment. We found a couple of two wheeled trucks and got alot of packages out, but the only place to put them was in the street and they were being looted by the civilian population almost as quickly as we were bringing them out. There were some carboys of acid and cans of paraffin stacked up and by now the flames began to lick the stuff we were rescuing and any minute we felt the vessels of acid would explode. We decided we had done all we could and came out to protect the stuff in the street from the looters. The next warehouse to the burning one was untouched by the fire, but the doors were broken open. We went in and found an Aladins Cave. There were large crates of boxed chocolates, (which I presume had been intended for the Christmas trade), and thousands of bottles of whisky, gin, beer, claret and every drink you could want. It was a Customs Warehouse and these were in Bond. There was an order in force that all alcoholic drink was to have been destroyed some three weeks before and we had destroyed a lot in Kuala Lumpur before we left .

There were already a dozen or so men in the warehouse who had cartons on their heads. Some dashed out with their loot, others dropped it and ran past us into the street. We tried to fasten the doors on to the street but the locks were smashed. The rest of the men said they would fasten the doors from the inside and I was to keep the crowd at bay. The mob gradually came nearer and nearer to me and became menacing. I threatened them with my rifle and pushed the bolt home with a round in the breech.

The crowd behind was now forcing those infront to give way towards me. Many of them were women and children. I was about to fire over their heads when suddenly I heard the crack of rifle fire and then the sound of machine gun fire. I looked up and on the hillside going up to Fort Canning were a detachment of Indian troops. They must have seen that I would have been overwhelmed at any second, and opened fire on the rear of the crowd. One moment there were 500 potential looters facing me, and then the shots rang out and within seconds the street was empty.

I made my way back down the street to our Billet and reported to an Officer that there was enough drink in the warehouse to have the local population mad drunk by midnight.

We went to the front of the Engineers Building and I said, "It is in the building next to the one on fire to the right". He said, "Is it safe out there?" He was very reluctant to leave the shelter and before we had any further chance to discuss anything, I heard the whistle of another shell. It made a direct hit on the building we were discussing and the whole warehouse disintegrated and fire leapt into the sky. I was very sad to think of all that drink being wasted when we were so thirsty.

I went back into our Billet Building feeling thoroughly frustrated and useless. I knew that nothing we could do would be of any use, and felt our fate was sealed. We would be Prisoners of War within a few days.

CHAPTER SIX

THE BEGINNING OF THE END

Three Signalmen, including myself, were detailed to go to the Main Post Office in Singapore and help in the manning of the switchboard there, which was the Main Link in ordinary times with all the world's telephone lines. On the day of the surrender of Singapore to the Japanese, February 14th 1942, we had been on duty for three days and nights along with two Eurasian girls, getting what sleep we could when we could. All around the Post Office, most of the buildings were damaged by bombs or by mortar fire, but the exchange itself was reinforced with a thick concrete roof and a layer of sandbags. From midday, on the last day before hostilities ceased, we were being telephoned to ask if the war was over, or to tell us the Japanese had arrived in their village and asking if it was correct that we had already surrendered.

Although things looked very hopeless, we had to refuse to hold any conversation with these callers, as they could well be Japanese trying to get information .

Around 3.00 p.m. on that afternoon the bombers came over and landed two or three direct hits on the Telephone Exchange. With great presence of mind, the girls dived under the table. The three of us tried to shield them by falling on top of them. When the dust and pieces of concrete had all settled, we were in no hurry to leave the cosy position we had taken up until the girls suggested that the immediate danger might be over for the moment.

Whilst they went to the cloakroom for a wash and dust down, we inspected the damage to the banks of the Automatic Exchange mechanism.

The bombs had landed on the flat roof of the building and had exploded before penetrating the roof altogether. However, there had been alot of plaster and concrete dislodged in amongst the Automatic Lines. The girls rejoined us very quickly and insisted on manning the Exchange whilst we cleared up the debris .

There were no windows in the part of the building we were in so until we went out to dump the rubble, we had not realised the extent of the damage around the area. All the buildings in the immediate vicinity were flattened and our Exchange was standing alone.

Half an hour later, and Officer came round to tell us of the Truce, but he was a little incoherent, so we rang the only line that seemed to be working, which, luckily was our H.Q. at Fort Canning, and they confirmed that there was a cease-fire.

The Head Postmaster came into the Exchange and sat at the desk we had been sheltering under, opened the draws and produced packets of Malayan Dollars. We could not have realised this at the time, but these would have been life savers if we had taken them. Never having been in this situation before we thought they would be useless after we had been taken prisoner. We did not realise that there would be ways of spending these small Dollar notes even after we got to prison. They could have bought us food, cigarettes or been used for bribery of our guards. We walked out on a million Dollars. The Postmaster also had another problem. He was a member of the Malayan Volunteer Force. He could surrender with the Services or be Interned as a Civilian .

We were told to muster at the Engineers Building where some of our Unit were staying. We took sad leave of the girls and wished them well as they had shown tremendous courage. They even offered to hide one of us if he could get to the convent where they lived. We telephoned them the next day and they assured us the Japanese had not harmed them, but asked them to stay on the Exchange.

I hated the fact that we had retreated 400 miles down the peninsular from Kuala Lumpur just to calmly surrender without a last ditch stand. We had no idea how we would be treated as, until then, the Japanese had not taken a large scale surrender. All rifles were to be stacked and surrendered the following day, February 16th 1942.

The following morning, a Japanese Officer came into the Engineers Building where we were billeted, and I was worried in case he examined the rifles, as most of us had knocked off the firing pin rendering them useless .

The orders of the Japanese were that we must march or walk to Changi Garrison which is about 15 miles from Singapore town. For the previous seven or eight days and nights the enemy had plastered us with heavy gunfire from Johore, air bombing strikes and latterly mortar fire. The very silence of the night after the surrender was somehow more nerve wracking than the row of the previous days and nights.

The journey to Changi was a humiliating experience. Many of the casualties were still unburied and the local population were very frightened and all wore handkerchiefs over their noses and mouths to try and minimise the stench of death which lay all around. Occasionally a Japanese soldier would fire a shot at a Chinese looter.

We had to carry all of our possessions with us and also take some kitchen utensils. All my personal possessions and most of my clothing, other than what I stood up in, was left behind when I left the last camp, as I had expected to go back there that night.

Over the last week I'd had very little food except what I had managed to scrounge from other units. I suppose I was fortunate to lose most of my kit when I did, as I would have lost it later anyway. It was a long and painful march to Changi which had been a large Military Garrison Barracks for many years. It covered quite a few acres and was on the side of the Strait separating Singapore from Malaya. The Signals were given the Garrison Theatre as their Billet.

I met up again with many of the men of my Unit of whom I had not seen since leaving Singapore for Kuala Lumpur. Any food which had been brought into Changi either by individuals or by Units was pooled for the benefit of the whole unit of Signals. We had a very small allocation the first night as we scattered amongst other sections and did not have the opportunity to amass anything in the way of rations .

At this stage the Japanese refused to provide any food, equipment, bedding or medical supplies. We had to improvise with any material that was laying around the barrack blocks. Mosquito nets had mostly been discarded, and many of us had little more than a blanket and the clothes we had on when we were captured. Weary and dispirited, I found myself a space on the floor of the stage and was surrounded by sleeping bodies in every square foot space.

During the night I was awakened by the pressure of a boot on my nose and realised it was someone trying to get to an exit. I thought if I call out or move the owner of the foot would most likely bring the other foot down with much more force. I bore the pain and indignity, sat up and waited for him to come back and settle down.

Daylight came at 6.00 o'clock every morning and dusk was six in the evening. This morning I awoke at daylight and looked across towards the Johore Straits. Japanese ships were passing almost stem to stern. There were little ships with a Kamikaze plane on the deck, destroyers, battleships, aircraft carriers, supply boats and troop carriers. All of these carried planes on deck. On the smaller ships and boats there was no way that the planes could land back on the ship once launched. This procession of warships went on almost continually for the whole of the daylight hours .

My main concern now was to get my name on to every survivors list that were being compiled by our Commanding Officers. At this stage we had very little contact with our captors as the guards were mainly on the perimeter limits. One of our first lessons was that if you failed to bow when you met them, you would receive a beating up. We rapidly learnt to do a Nippon Bow wherever necessary.

There was no mains water running at this stage as the mains had been blown up by the shelling and bombing. What water there was available was from storage tanks set in the ground in various places in the area. It had always puzzled me that of all the contingencies which had not been thought of, the chances of this being required in an emergency would seem remote. However, it was a tremendous help to us as we were able to use this for drinking if it was boiled. The ration was about one and a half pints a day including tea.

The first few days as a Prisoner of War were spent trying to locate old friends for news of men of our own sections. I had a pack of playing cards and spent hours playing cards for money we did not have. During these games the dealer always shuffled the cards and had them cut before dealing. I dealt in my turn and the first caller called abundance, which meant he gambled to take all the tricks. The next player called abundance on Trumps which is a higher call and took precedence over the previous call. The third player called abundance declared which meant he was prepared to put his hand down on the table. I then picked up my own hand and to my astonishment I had a complete suit of thirteen. I had dealt from a shuffled pack of cards four complete suits on suit to each player. A chance in a million.

After a week or more we were still living on the food which various individuals and sections had brought in with them and the stored water was now coming to an end. Rumours of all kinds were rife within the Camp both good and bad, but more were bad than good. The Japanese had promised they would provide us with some food in early April, but by now the poor diet and lack of hygiene and no medical supplies was beginning to take its toll. Men were going down with dysentery, dengue fever and malaria and with very limited medication and no proper hospital the spread of disease was very rapid.

During the retreat from Kuala Lumpur I only occasionally had the chance to get a wash or a change of clothes and most nights we had to be ready to move at once and so I slept wherever I was, usually on the floor. By this time everyone was beginning to get bored and some men were breaking out through the wire to get food off the local people. The Sikhs had joined the Japanese forces and were being used as guards at the Prison Camps. They were very afraid of their Japanese allies and so gave anyone they caught outside the perimeter some terrible beatings.

We knew when someone had gone over the wire as first one, then another dog would start to bark and there would be much activity amongst the guards with an occasional shot fired. The thought of escape was only considered by a few men who were dark skinned and spoke a local language. Anyone who was European would have been quickly picked up and probably executed.

Food was now becoming the chief topic of conversation. Everyone except a few who were working in the cookhouses was now feeling hungry for 24 hours a day. We had the use of a swimming pool which was a boarded off area of the Straits which contained sea water. I spent a lot of time in the water and although the salt water was painful on the raw areas of my feet which had not recovered from the outbreak of Tinia, they began to heal. I was also able to walk around with bare feet .

The Japs were now asking for skilled men to work in Singapore on restoring the water supply and electricity. Parties began to be made up and went into Singapore under Jap guards and in our captured trucks .

We were in the pool one morning when a boat with two men aboard rowed across from the Island and brought bananas and dried fish. Some men bought a few of these with money that they had brought in with them. The Japanese guards who were on the roof of the large barracks block, spotted the boat and opened fire with a machine gun. One of the men jumped out of the boat but was hit whilst swimming away. His body was washed ashore two days later and we buried it in the compound. The other man rowed away frantically and then disappeared into the bottom of the boat. The guards came and took the fruit away from the men who had bought it but took no further action.

There were coconut palms and also two large mango trees around the perimeter of what had been the old Garrison Cricket field. I spotted two or three mangoes which looked like they might fall off any day. If anyone was seen climbing any tree within the camp it invited a burst of machine gun fire from the roof of the barrack block. The next few day I spent all available time underneath the trees hoping a breeze would dislodge the ripe fruit and hoping no-one else would notice why I was around there. On the third day a tribe of monkeys came along and I watched with bitter disappointment as they picked the mangos, ate them and threw the stones in my direction.

My first spell in hospital at Changi was in early June 1942 for 19 days with dysentery, there was very little the doctors could do except give you a dose of Castor Oil which at least made you run faster to the loo. The medical stores available were almost nil. According to some notes I had kept although I had only left hospital on June 24th and discharged as cured, I was back again with dysentery from July 5th to August 27th .

During those early days of being a Prisoner of War, most of us were trying to convince ourselves that we would probably stay for a maximum of a year, and the rumours that floated around were almost always of victories both on land and sea. During my stay in hospital, I bought a jar of jam from a patient and when I got out of hospital

I met a friend who had acquired a tin of condensed milk. We agreed to meet each evening for three evenings and partake of the tremendous luxury of jam and milk for supper. We had to avoid letting any other person see us or we would have to put the jar down our shirts or risk losing it. The rations now being allowed us in Changi were totally inadequate and according to all medical textbooks our total intake of food was not sufficient to keep us alive, but this was not true as I am here to tell the story.

On September 1st 1942, the Japanese Commander called on our Camp Commandant and showed him a piece of paper calling on every man in the camp to sign a pledge that he would not attempt to escape from any Japanese Prison Camp. There were no concessions offered in return for the pledge. Our Officers refused to sign and also refused to present these papers to the men. The Commandant the threatened to force all the prisoners to make their own way up to Selarang Square and they would be kept there until we had all signed the documents. Under such pressure, our Commander said he would present the pieces of paper to all men for their signature and leave the decision as to whether they signed or not to each individual. No-one signed them except three men who were under confinement for stealing drugs. We were then given an ultimatum that if the forms were not signed by 4.00 o'clock that afternoon we must all make our way up to Selarang Square. This included those in hospital with the exception of those who were bedridden .

The deadline for everyone to be there was 11.00 a.m. on the following morning. The distance for most of us was about a mile or two but besides carrying all our possessions, we also had to take as much as we could carry in the way of cooking utensils, spades, pickaxes and chunkels. The mood of most men was really remarkably cheerful in view of what lay ahead. There was one Scot who put on full dress Kilt, sporran and bonnet and had obtained four small wheels and had made himself a little cart on which he had loaded everything he possessed. Lodged on the top was a very fine China Po which was carefully tied on with string and he marched with head held up high playing the bagpipes .

By 11.00 o'clock there were sixteen thousand men packed into this small area. Also four goats and ten chickens which were somehow smuggled in. We were allowed to bring one truck to carry the large cooking cauldrons and a few medical supplies and stretchers. By 11.15

a.m. the area was surrounded by a single strand of barbed wire and we were warned not to step outside the wire. Machine guns were mounted at all four corners of the square giving a clear view along the outer road on all four sides. The Japanese Commander set up a Headquarters in a hut at one end of the area which had no Barrack Block on it and gave him a clear view of what was going on within the area. The only lavatories were one or two at each end and on each floor of the buildings. The only place additional "Boreholes" could be located was by digging through the concrete on the Parade Ground. Our first meal was in the evening and consisted of a small cupful of cooked rice.

Every square foot of space including all the floor space in the Barrack Blocks was covered by people or an essential piece of equipment. During the evening someone ventured a couple of steps over the wire to try to recapture one of the chickens. He was immediately set upon by the guards, beaten up and literally thrown back over the wire with a warning that the excursion outside the wire would be met by a hail of machine gun fire. Darkness fell about six and apart from the noise of the digging through the concrete, everything was entirely quiet.

When the men decided to bed down for the night, the space available to lie down was so limited that we could not stretch our legs out. I as well as a few thousand more slept on the concrete, but by this time the concrete was not so hard as it appeared to be when we were forced to sleep on the floor. As the weary night wore on more and more men were wanting to use the latrines and the queue got longer and longer. Fortunately the night was fine and there was a full moon. We had no idea how long the Japanese were going to keep us penned in like cattle. Even at this stage people were falling ill and we were not allowed to move them out.

The second evening of our stay was enlivened by a concert performed from the truck which we had been allowed to bring in. We started some community singing and the God Save The King was sung with probably more fervour than it had ever been sung before. The guards recognised the song and produced a megaphone and made dire threats if we sung it again. One look at the activity at each machine gun post persuaded us that we would change the tune. We switched to "Land of Hope and Glory". This then became the substitute for the National Anthem at most concerts.

The third day saw more cases of acute illness and two deaths.

The Japanese Commanding Officer sent for our Commanding Officer and made him stand to attention during the negotiations which were held in full view of the troops. The ultimatum was that if we did not sign the Parole Document the following day, the doctors, orderlies and all patients from the hospital would be forced to somehow and without ambulances make their way to Selarang Square as best they could. This included the bedridden as well. They had already discharged two people from the hospital and sent them to join us in an ambulance and then refused to let the ambulance go back. No-one was to remain in the hospital. Had our Officers refused to sign there would have been well over a hundred deaths of these patients whilst on their way to the Square. No-one was in hospital unless they were very seriously ill anyway.

It was decided by our Commanding Officer that to avoid so many deaths the troops were ordered to sign the Parole Papers. The fact that we had been ordered to sign the parole by our Officers meant that we were covered against any Courts Martial which may occur when we were set free .

The papers with the text of the parole promise (Not to attempt to escape) on them were distributed individually for us to sign. As by this time very few men had any sort of writing instrument in their possession the whole procedure took a very long time, but eventually 16,000 signed papers were delivered back to the Japanese. Had they checked the names which were signed they would have had some difficulty in tracing Mickey Mouse of the Argyll and Sutherland Highlanders or I.M.A. Ramm of the Derbyshire Regiment or even U. Bastard of the Royal Corps of Signals.

On the fourth day after being forced into Selarang Square, we were told to return to the areas we had come from. Many of the men had contracted dysentery, malaria, ulcers etc during the stay in Selarang Square because of the fact that we had all been forced to be in close contact with everybody else. Many men had to be carried back on stretchers to the areas and some taken straight to the hospital area. After four days with only one small ration if rice each day, everyone was weakened by their experience .

We all felt, although we had signed, we had no obligation to keep the parole terms and we had won a moral victory over the enemy and perhaps felt better for having made the stand.

Shortly after this incident I was ordered to report to Temple Hill which was the old Headquarters of Far Eastern Command and a group of palatial buildings which had a wonderful view overlooking the whole of Singapore Sea Front and Harbour. The high ranking Officers who survived the war were there in rather less opulent circumstances than before the surrender. However, to us ordinary soldiers who were detailed to look after them, and keep the area clean and tidy, it was a plum job. We were able to get small extras in the way of food and accommodation. Some careless Officer may leave a half tin of jam which really should have been handed in when we first surrendered, lying around and after all we were there to tidy up. It would have been a disaster if the ants had eaten it. It would be hidden until the hue and cry was over and then shared out amongst us.

In the evenings we would take walks round the block in twos and threes and even in the circumstances we would appreciate the sunsets and the moon riding high over the bay.

By now tobacco was becoming scarce and cigarettes almost non-existent. Loose tobacco and papers to roll your own cigarettes were very valuable and could be traded for someones meal. One evening four of us were strolling round the grounds as it was a beautiful night. In front of us were three Officers one of whom was smoking a cigar. We kept a reasonable distance behind them. No-one spoke but each knew that we were all wondering how long it would be before the cigar end would be discarded. Three times we walked slowly round the block of buildings hoping he would throw the cigar end down before they went inside. Just as they reached the front entrance to their quarters, the smoker dropped the butt on to the ground. We all stopped and waited like athletes on their starting blocks to make a dash for the remains as soon as the trio had gone into the building. However, the smoker carefully threw the end down in front of him and crushed it into the ground. If we could have obtained a small piece of paper we could have had perhaps three puffs each with the remains of that cigar.

The Japanese Artillery fire and bombing raids just before the Capitulation had destroyed most of the Godowns (warehouses) in the Singapore Dock area. In amongst these buildings were some Cold Store Deep Freeze stores where meat was kept hung in full carcasses. The electric power had been off for some time and it was realised that the contents would be useless by the time repairs could be carried out. I was detailed for a work party to collect two whole carcasses and bring them back to our camp for our consumption. There was of course no power available to help load these onto the truck.

They were still very hard and frozen, and apart from the weight, difficult to get a hold on. Two of the men on the job were butchers and they borrowed a large axe. They first split the carcasses down the backbone as they hung. We only had cotton shorts and shirts on and it was bitterly cold in the freezers. As the men chopped, small pieces of hard frozen meat fell on the floor. As each small chip fell, we pounced on it and stuffed them into our mouths, dirt and sawdust as well. By the time we had sucked the ice off the meat would be no bigger than a marble. The whole carcasses were cut into manageable pieces and loaded onto the truck. I managed to grab a dozen or so small pieces. My mouth was frozen inside and I could not taste what it was like but we knew even those small bits were worth something to us .

The Japanese guards enjoyed the spectacle of their prisoners grabbing at morsels of meat like vultures round a killed beast. This was part of the cost of survival. The two carcasses were to be divided amongst some 30,000 men. We never noticed any taste of meat in the stewed vegetables and rice which was served up at night for our meal.

Before our surrender, an armaments store was denied by blowing it up and the remains were within the barracks at Changi. This was in a wet area of the barracks and there were many craters and puddles caused by the explosion. These were breeding places for mosquitos and the Japs ordered that a work party should be organised to try and prevent an outbreak of malaria in Singapore. This was put in charge of two men who appeared to be the oldest men taken prisoner. They had been, I understand, in the Malayan Volunteer Force, and had decided to be taken Prisoners of War rather than Civilian Internees.

They were specialists in malarial control in civilian life and worked for the Malayan authorities. I was put on this detail and was glad to be away from the squalor of the camp itself. This was known as the Anti-Malarial Squad, and we were furnished with a chunkel each (this is used as a spade for filling in the craters). The two men became known as "Anti Malaria and Uncle Chunkel!" We filled the larger craters with the surrounding earth. The Japanese had been asked to provide us with any old engine oil from Singapore garages. Small branches were cut from the bushes and dipped in th oil and then dragged through the puddles. This left a film of oil floating on the top of the water and prevented the Mosquito eggs hatching. This was very effective and was repeated about every four or five days during the rainy season.

We were allowed to swim in an area of the sea which was fenced off with railings to the depth of the pool to prevent large fish or octopus getting in. The water was not very clean but it was an opportunity to have a good soak and wash. I was in the water one day and came face to face with a huge King Turtle. It completely ignored the swimmers and according to the Regular Army me it had been in there ever since the pool was built and seemed to enjoy human company.

Whilst in the Army I had maintained a regular weight of 11 stones but I left hospital weighing 8 stones. The criteria for discharge from Hospital was if you had no more than three motions a day you were fit for the outside world. Owing to the lack of pressure in the water mains the flush toilets could only be used at certain times of the night. This meant that we had to have latrines in a small room at the end of the building. These consisted of five gallon drums with the tops cut away and two wooden slats across. The woodwork became infested with what we knew as bed bugs. These attacked soon after you had sat down and drew blood with numerous bites in places best left unbitten. The smell was appalling, but we became used to the stench of rotting flesh from ulcers etc.

I was back in hospital with dysentery in October 1942, When whatever food we ate was not retained long enough for the nourishment to be extracted by the system. All the rice we were receiving in rations was 'polished'. That is the outside husk was extracted from the rice. Unfortunately this meant that the main nutrient in the rice was missing. The Doctors asked the Japanese if we could be given the polishings or husks. These were served separately and taken as medicine. Floating on the top of half a pint of 'Rice Polishings' would be drowned weevils. Horrible as this was if we could get some nourishment from it we would swallow the mixture, weevils and all. We ate them and cheered ourselves with the idea that they served as a meat ration. The vegetables we were getting were mostly sweet potato tops which was the foliage of the plant before the tubers had formed. Our need for some green vegetable was so urgent that we could not wait for the tubers to grow.

The Japanese ordered some of the Officers to move into the

top story of the building being used as a Hospital block. Most of the buildings in Changi barracks were purpose built for the Garrison Troops stationed there before the war. Each floor had an open balcony.

We in the hospital were very interested to see that what they had been able to bring into the camp and retain after nine months in captivity.

The party arrived with a large trailer which was piled high with cabin trunks, suit cases, large tin clothes lockers and various beds and bedding. A strong set of blocks and tackle was fastened to a beam on the roof and the long haul began with the larger items first and after some arguments as to whose goods should go up first. The Australians were getting more and more annoyed at the amount of possessions the Officers had been able to salvage as against other ranks who had to leave everything behind except what they could carry themselves. The breaking point came when a large steel locker was attached to the rope ready for a manual long haul to the top story. I saw one of the men who were doing the hauling look over the balcony as the load was about ten feet from the ground. They checked no one was underneath and let go of the rope. Suddenly there was a loud shout of keep clear and the locker went down at a very fast pace and landed on one corner and although it was locked it burst open and scattered the contents under the gaze of the Australians. According to the Officers this was supposed to contain Regimental books and Medical supplies. The fatigue party were astonished to see tins of fruit and corned beef and other tinned foods which were supposed to have been handed in to the pool for the whole camp. They insisted that there must have been some mistake and no one knew it contained any food. However, the men picked all the tinned food up and took it to the hospital kitchen and the officers were powerless to object. Perhaps not every tin reached the stores!

Whilst I was in the hospital in Changi I was intrigued and baffled by a demonstration of mind reading by a man named Piddington. We were in a Barrack Building three storeys high with a balcony all the way round each floor.

The orderlies organised it so that one end of the ward was cleared of beds and anyone who was fit to get up was sat on the beds. A rough circle was formed and Piddington was brought into the circle. He spoke to the wardmaster telling him to arrange any kind of action that he (Piddington) must perform on his return to the ward. He was then accompanied by two of the patients to remain out of our sight and hearing on the balcony. The two patients were both men we knew to have no connection with the performer before and they had never seen or heard of Piddington before.

As I remember it all the patients were then asked to suggest what tasks Piddington was to perform on his return. We took some ten minutes in which people were suggesting various actions. The final scene was that Piddington was to approach one man who had an Army shirt on and get from his top right hand pocket a cigarette lighter (which belonged to someone else) give the lighter to another patient then choose someone to give him a cigarette to give to a third party and he was then to light the cigarette he had just given the patient.

Piddington was then asked to return to the ward and perform his allotted tasks. He walked in to absolute silence. Pondered for a time and then went across to a man who also had a shirt on with breast pockets. He then felt if there was any article in that pocket. There was not so he felt his right hand trouser pocket and found a lighter there. He examined and felt the lighter in his hand and decided it was not right and handed it back to its owner. He then went to the man who had the correct lighter, took it from his top pocket and went to another Doctor, asked him for a cigarette which he produced and proceeded to ask the man with the lighter to give him a light.

The whole episode was enacted in complete silence and without any help from anyone. The only person present who was not known to all those present was Piddington who was living in another ward away from our block. In later years this man performed in many acts of Telepathy on television, radio and the theatre. Sadly he died in early 1991. This could not have been performed in a more difficult situation and I have always maintained that he was genuine and had powers not given to any else .

CHAPTER SEVEN

BY GOODS TRAIN TO THAILAND

The Japanese High Command called for volunteers to go up-country to Thailand to build a railway.

A notice went up on the Notice Board which read something like this: The IMPERIAL JAPANESE ARMY are to build a railway going through Siam to Burma. Prisoners are asked to volunteer to go to camps in Siam where the work will be easy and there will be three days work followed by two days rest in a holiday camp. The Concert Party will be welcome to go along with the rest of the party."

Six hundred men were required for the party which was designated "F" Force. Few of the other ranks believed that it would be anything other than a work party and as usual my name was on the list to go in spite of the fact that I had only just left hospital. I did not try to get out of the detail as I followed my usual practice of not trying to get out of any detail as the next assignment might be worse. We were told by the Japanese to take everything with us that we could carry ourselves and to parade in Changi village at 3.00 a.m. on the morning of 27th April 1943.

Trucks were waiting to take us to Singapore station. This was the first time I had been in a motor vehicle or out of Changi barracks since the Capitulation. From what I could see out of the rear of the truck, very little had been done to restoring the services or repairing the roads in Singapore town.

When we arrived at Singapore station and the trucks were being unloaded, it was clear that the Officers had taken the Japanese order seriously. I was amazed to see being dumped in the station yard a big drum, a piano and a portable church organ and also a varied array of cloth for concert scenery backdrop. The few Officers who were to go with us all appeared to have two suitcases each and one even had an Army Greatcoat and another had a trunk.

As we arrived, not at the station platform, but in the goods yards of Singapore station all the gear we had was off-loaded on to the ground. This meant that the piano had to be lifted by hand from the ground to the wagon and this was no easy task as many of us were newly out of hospital. We were also allocated some large cooking utensils to take care of through the journey. The train was made of steel sided covered wagons normally used for transporting rice in sacks. The railway trucks had sliding doors and no ventilation. These had to be loaded under Japanese Officers supervision with kitbags, haversacks, cooking utensils and field kitchens.

We, the human cargo, then had to make do with what space was left, which meant clambering over all the bric-a-brac on the floor of the wagon. About twenty men were allocated to each truck. We lived in these wagons night and day for six or seven days. One of the wagons must have been lumbered with the piano and the big drum.

It was probably nine or ten in the morning before we steamed out of the siding onto the main line. This was the start of a journey of hunger, stifling heat, comparative cold nights and misery for six hundred already debilitated men. By midday the sides of the metal trucks were too hot to lean against and the atmosphere within them was stinking, as only a limited number of men could be near the doors at any one time for some fresh air. The last food we had was the previous evening and apart from water from our own water bottles, we'd had no food over the past ten hours.

During the morning we were shunted into sidings to allow troop trains through but we were not allowed to get out of the trucks. We stopped at a station about midday and were given a drink of tea with no milk or sugar and allowed off the train to relieve ourselves and stretch our legs. We were also provided with a ladle full of sloppy rice and greens with perhaps an odd piece of meat if you were lucky. We had more stops in the jungle to take on logs for fuel for the engine, and at some of these we were allowed to get out and have a short walk. On some of these stops we were given tea.

Nightfall came and still we had no more food. As the sun went down the stifling heat in the trucks gradually turned to cold and we huddled together in blankets to get some warmth. With the cargo we had aboard we could not stretch out to sleep, but slept resting against whatever we found most comfortable. By dawn we had only had one bite of food in the last 36 hours. Dawn to me was always a time to hope for a better day and a breath of fresh air, the air and the rising sun seemed to combine to make life worth living after all.

The next stop was outside Kuala Lumpur, where we were given a cup of tea and some stewed rice. Even as early as this dysentery was beginning to take its toll and no-one had washed mess tins or hands for two days. Sand and dust was constantly being blown in through the open doors of the rice trucks. We arrived at Penang and were shunted into a goods yard and allowed to get out of the trucks, some rice and stew was provided by the Japanese and eagerly gobbled up by us hungry men .

News of our arrival must have reached the natives and very soon a swarm of naked little children with grossly swollen bellies and eyes came begging for food and if you turned your head a tiny fist would dive into your mess tin and grab what they could of your sparse meal. I had finished my food before they arrived but I wondered how I would have reacted had these poor kids arrived before I had eaten.

By now we were feeling the effects, not only of being continually hungry but also the lack of exercise and the sheer boredom of life in a railway truck. Most of the journey was now through thick forest and the atmosphere was more oppressive.

An extra engine had been put on at Penang and on the gradients a third engine pushed from the rear. These needed to take on wood for fuel and water and we were glad of the extra stops this afforded us to go into the scrub.

I had a small amount of tea stored in the only sock I still possessed. At one stop four of us each poured a cupful of water into a mess tin from our water bottles. We built a small fire of sticks and got a light from the engine driver, from the fire to boil the water. We just had time to dip the tea sock into the water when the Jap guard came and ordered us back into our wagon. However, we managed to share the tea before we got back on the train. I then hung the tea sock just inside our wagon to dry for the next stop.

The next halt was beside a stream and afforded us an opportunity to refill our bottles and put some in the mess tin. We had just got the fire going when the Jap guard indicated he would like to see us back in the truck quickly. We tried to make him understand that the water was not yet boiling, but he was going to take a kick at the mess tin, fire and sock, so we grabbed the sock and the mess tin and scrambled under the train to the other side and jumped into our wagon. By the time he had crawled after us, hampered by his rifle and his equipment we had climbed into our trucks and were out of sight. As everyone was aboard the train, he left us to catch his coach at the rear of the train .

We were now not very far away from the border with Thailand. The first indication of this was when we were approached by Money Changers every time we slowed down or stopped. It began out in the country with men running beside the line with various offers of exchange rates to change Malayan Dollars for Thailand Bahts. The problem was sometimes the train slowed and then picked up speed rapidly before the transaction finished and one of the traders could be left either with none or both currencies.

As we got nearer to the Thailand border the rates of exchange got better and better until they were more than double the original offers by the Jungle Boys. The only money most of us had to change was what we had brought into Changi. Some men had amassed extra money by sneaking out of camp at Changi and dealing with the local population or by buying food and selling watches or other valuables. This wealth had been amassed at the risk of getting shot for being outside the camp. I seemed to lose all sense of time and the only difference between night and day was, it was dark from 6.00 p.m. to 6.00 a.m. We made various stops in Thailand but there was not always any food or drink available.

The railway engines were huge and were all wood burning. Logs were cut in the forest and stacked in metre high piles beside the track and the driver just stopped and picked up a tender full whenever they were needed. We were often shunted into sidings to allow munitions trains through which would be bound for the Burma front. Sometimes truck loads of horses and wagons with large but very old cannon on them. We were later to encounter these up country.

It was not safe to drink water unless it was boiled or came from a well, so we sometimes got the driver to blow water from the boiler into our mess tins. It was a horrible rusty colour but was better than nothing .

Eventually about the sixth day of our journey we arrived at a town called Bam Pong. By this time many men were unable to walk and some were semi-conscious suffering from starvation, dysentery or malaria. We had to make stretchers from old rice sacks and bamboo poles or blankets. Few of us were strong enough to lower a stretcher down gently from a height of four or five feet from wagon to floor.

Weary, hungry and thirsty we off loaded all our kit and helped those who were too sick to walk. These wagons had been our homes for the past six days and nights and were now filthy so we felt glad to get out of them. The stench of sweaty clothing, sick men and incontinence was overpowering. We had worn the same garments day and night for a week and rarely had we the opportunity even to wash our hands. Little did we realise that the next part of the journey was to be worse but instead of riding we would be walking.

Everything was gathered together and in addition to our own kit, we had the kitchen utensils to take with us. We were not allowed any motor transport. The order was given to move and with Japanese guards infront, behind and on both sides of the column of men, we staggered up the road which was narrow but had a good surface.

In spite of the guards the Thai people approached us with gifts of fruit and raw eggs. They risked a beating from the Japs but never the less I got two eggs and with a quick bite and an intake of breath I bit the tops off and sucked out the contents and by then there was little the Japs could do about it. I was also lucky in getting some bread and two tomatoes. The nourishment coupled with gratefulness for this kindness and hospitality of these poor people at the risk of a beating helped to give me new hope of mankind. I also remember looking back towards the station and seeing in the middle of an open space one very lonely piano and one big drum. They had to be abandoned after all our efforts at loading and unloading them. Again more about the piano later.

1

2

4

9

10

We marched through the town and for another two miles along this road and came to a large camp site. One side of the area was occupied by priests with saffron coloured robes and shaven heads.

They all looked so clean and well dressed that they made a sharp contrast to our dirty, bedraggled state. In the centre of the area we were to occupy was a huge pile of clothes, kit bags, haversacks and all manner of things which had been discarded by the previous Prisoners of War who had gone before us. This heap was already twenty feet high. On the morrow we would no doubt be adding to that pile. It astonished me to see what some men decided was essential but I could well understand how precious articles connected with home and of sentimental value were hard to just throw as high as you could to the top of the pile of the past.

The Japanese told us that we would be leaving the following day on foot for a camp nearer the Burma Railway and as the roads would be mostly along jungle paths we were to take the absolute minimum kit. We must also carry everything we needed for cooking at each stopover. Hence again the decision had to be made as to what you considered essential and what had to be discarded to the heap.

The 2nd May 1943 was spent sorting out who should carry the various camp stores. We were also subjected to a very cursory medical inspection. If you could stand on two feet you were considered fit to march. We had two, by comparison, quite good meals during that day and we were ordered to parade at 5.00 p.m. with all we had to carry. We were counted and checked and rechecked by the Japanese guards and eventually moved off at 7.00 p.m.

CHAPTER EIGHT

TREKKING THROUGH THE JUNGLE

It was a bright moonlit night. The first few miles were through lovely country and on a fairly good road. It was not very long before the road became a track and then nothing more than a forest pathway. This meant we had to walk in single file and as I was helping to carry a large cooking pan which could not be carried by one man, in some parts we had to walk sideways.

The pattern of the march over the next six nights was, we marched for about 55 minutes and rested for 5 minutes in each hour with a break of about half an hour around midnight. The main occupation during the break was to burst blisters on the feet and let some air get to them. At dawn we usually stopped in a clearing in the jungle and some fifteen to twenty men would be detailed to prepare a meal of whatever the Japs provided. The meal was nearly always the same, a watery soup with a small amount of meat and some various vegetable. This meant getting sticks and timber for the fires. I was not detailed the first morning for any duties so, as soon as the order came that we had done our nights march, I looked around and found a suitable bush and poked about in the undergrowth with a stick to clear the area of snakes, scorpions and other crawlers. I then lay down fully dressed except for boots and these I tied to my waist and also strapped my haversack to my legs.

All these precautions were necessary as there were a lot of Thai's around who would steal your blanket off your back and you would not realise until much later that it had disappeared. I found it difficult to sleep in spite of being footsore and weary after the nights trek. All the time up to midday the heat was greater and greater and having to sleep covered up for protection from snakes and ants and other insects made it very uncomfortable.

Breakfast consisted of a cupful of sloppy rice with a few vegetables thrown in and served about 11.00 a.m. I was still suffering with septic wounds on the soles of my feet and the only help available was a hot footbath with a little bit of anti-septic in. Not enough water was available for a wash so once again we were beginning to feel uncomfortably filthy. There was a well nearby but we had to take our turn with the villagers to use it and what we did get up was only sufficient for drinking purposes and the cookhouse. Most of the local population were very kind and friendly and were quite willing to allow us to use their well .

This meant that the Japanese guards were always very suspicious of their motives and went out of their way to chase them away from talking to us. Before starting the next nights trek, we had a second cup of rice, only the second in the last twelve hours. We were ordered to be ready to march off again by 7.00 p.m. and after two or three roll calls we were once more on the jungle trail. The bush was now getting denser and denser and we had to duck to avoid overhead branches and to step over the tree roots. This was very difficult with a large haversack on your back and also carrying the cooking gear.

Again when the nights march was over we crawled into the bushed and I fell asleep at once and when the call for breakfast came (this was the beating of a bucket with a bamboo stick) it was really quite pathetic to see, crawling out of the bushes, what looked like bundles of old clothes on scarecrows limping and staggering to get to a meal which was just another bowl of rice. We were obviously getting thinner and thinner and many were not fit to go on. This meant that after a few miles there would be a shout from the rear Japanese guard, the column would be brought to a halt and two men would go back and pick up the fallen comrade. This meant that for most of the night we would have two or three people to carry, on makeshift stretchers. The carry was shared by all who were in better condition than those on the stretchers .

The third night the Japanese guards called us together before we set off. "Tonight we go through tiger country. Much danger to all. If Japanese guard says 'Sing' you sing loud and frighten tigers away," that was an order .

About midnight the mist came down over the trees and into the forest and the steam came up from the ground but leaving a "no mist land" in between and we came to a track which was wide enough to take a yak cart and a pair of yaks. The mist slowly dispersed and the moon came out and made the scene eerily beautiful and for some reason the calls of animals and birds which normally go on all night, were hushed. I was almost lost in the beauty of it amongst all our suffering. I was brought back to earth by a frantic howl from somewhere in the trees which sounded like a tiger roaring. Then came a far more frantic howl from the Japanese guard. "Sing. Sing all men. Sing loud tigers. Tigers!" Everyone broke into song, from "She'll be coming down the mountain" to "Bless 'em all" and "God Save The King".

The roars appeared to be coming from the jungle on the right of the column. Everyone veered to the left of the road and the Japanese made it their business to have British troops between them and the tiger as the roaring seemed to get more and more ferocious.

I noticed that there was a very strong smell of burning hoof. Just off the road in a clearing was an empty yak cart and to one side was a roaring fire being kept roaring by bellows made of yak skin. Two men were holding the head of a yak and a blacksmith was fitting a new pair of shoes which the yak did not approve of and every so often gave a terrific roar. So much for tiger country. This episode livened up the night and we went the next few miles in quite a cheerful mood .

We were now on a long straight road raised above the swamps or paddy fields on either side. It was a dirt track and just about wide enough for a vehicle to use. This meant when we took our break there were no trees to lean our packs against whilst resting. My feet were now worse than when we started the march, and the holes in the soles of my feet were growing larger and larger. I still had a pair of boots but no socks and the boots were beginning to fall apart at the seams and the sole was very thin. By this time almost all our medical supplies were used up and apart from trying to wash my feet at the daytime stop there was nothing I could do to remove the pain when walking.

If I lay down to rest at the break times when we had a stop of five minutes in each hour, the weight of the large pack on my back was now more than I could raise. Without the trees to clamber up from the prone position the knee muscles would not respond to my commands. On the other hand, if I took the pack off and laid it down, I could not lift it back onto my shoulders when we had to move off again. Another problem was if I took the weight off my feet whilst resting I had to go through an enormous pain barrier each time I put the weight back onto my feet.

The human column now stretched some quarter of a mile from the front guard to the rear guard and we could proceed as we wished between the two. I decided rather than endure the pain of the first hundred yards or so after a rest I would start at the head of the column after each break and then as we walked the next stage, I would gradually fall further and further to the rear of the column and keep walking slowly without a rest. By the time the five minute rest was over I would be at the head of the column again and did not go through the agony of restarting.

Later during the very early hours of the morning the moon was obscured by cloud and mist. We staggered along as near to the centre of the road as we could as we knew there was a drop of ten of fifteen feet down a steep embankment and no-one would know where you had gone, and to scramble back up would be very difficult.

We heard in the distance, and apparently approaching us from the rear, what sounded like the cracking of whips and the clanking of chains. As these noises became louder they were accompanied by shouts in both Japanese and English. Suddenly out of the gloom we saw horses heads appear and these were pulling old iron tyred field guns with men riding the horses and others riding where they could on the cannons. Our only escape from being run over by the horses or cannon wheels was to scramble down the steep sides of the road and wait until the column had passed. When the dust and noise had settled, we scrambled back onto the road but there was no way of knowing if all had got back. Again out of the darkness came a column of marching Japanese soldiers. They deliberately spread themselves over the full width of the road, and we were forced to again fall down the banking or risk a clout with a rifle butt .

At times the soldiers had to man handle the wheels of the cannon to get them out of ruts or over some bad roadway. They demanded that we helped them and yelled all sorts of oaths and threats at us, but they dared not venture down the banking where we were all clinging desperately to tufts of grass to save a fall to the bottom.

Eventually, all was quiet and we ventured to re-appear onto the road and resumed the weary plod on through the night. Although this was a frightening episode, it again broke the monotony of the night and as we appeared to have suffered no casualties, no harm was done.

The following morning as dawn broke and the sun came up, the mist remained about waist high. It was like being detached from the earth and floating in mist of tremendous beauty. The hills were surrounded by mist rolling up the sides as if caressing them. Myriads of shiny cobwebs hung on the trees with tiny droplets of water tracing every strand of the webs and all the creatures of the dawn began to give welcome to the new day.

Then suddenly I was back to earth and conscious that below the mist I had two very painful feet, my knees were wobbly with the weight I was carrying which seemed twice as heavy as I could carry. Then again I took heart - dawn meant we had not far to go before we could fall down into the nearest bush and ignore the ants, the lizards, the snakes, the frogs and all creatures moving around us and fall into a deep sleep for four hours. The next vitally important event was the banging of the buckets to summon us to breakfast.

Each nights march saw more and more men fall by the wayside and more stretchers had to be improvised. We took turns carrying these men but it meant we were carrying not just the man but all his kit in addition to our own. The whole of the journey to where we had de-trained at Bam Pong had been through thick forest or jungle.

We desperately hoped we were nearing the end of our terrible march, and always optimistic, I thought any camp would be better than the painful marches we had been doing every night.

After increased harassment from the Siamese wanting to acquire any article we had and keeping a sharp look out for sneak thieves, we arrived on the outskirts on a town which we called The Three Pagodas. When we reached there in the early morning, the sun was shining directly onto the front of the pagodas and was a wonderful sight. During the morning some Thai girls came to the area and were selling tapioca and also a meat stew. They had a pole over their shoulder and a charcoal fire on a metal tray at one end and at the other bowls of freshly cooked food. They were selling the food to anyone who had the money to pay, alas not many had the money and when they realised we had no money they invited some of us to bring along our mess tins and shared out all they had left on the trays amongst those who had been unable to pay. This kindness was very genuine and a real morale booster.

The next day we arrived at what we thought was our destination for the time being at least. However, during the day the word went round that another party of 100 men was required to march further up country. I was one of the ten British Army men to be chosen. The other ninety were Australian or New Zealand troops. We were given a very cursory medical examination by the first Japanese Medical Officer we had seen. He pronounced me unfit to travel further because of the raw holes in the soles of both of my feet. There were many men in a worse condition than I was and our own Medical Officer said I would have to go. I kept to my resolution not to try and get out of a posting.

We set off the next day with only four Jap Guards. I had found a bamboo stick to help me walk but the strength to put one foot in front of the other to go forward became increasingly difficult and along with another man we fell behind the main party. The guard at the rear kept threatening us with his bayonet but it became more difficult even under the threat to move any faster.

Much to our surprise and relief he took POW numbers (these were written on a bit of inch wide ribbon and pinned on your hat or lapel), crossed them off his list and told us to go back to the camp we came from. We had already covered about three miles and passed two Japanese camps.

As soon as the rest of the party were out of sight we lay down under a tree and rested for some time and then set off back the same way we came, wondering what would happen as we walked back past the camps without guards and the rest of the party.

Here we were, left by the Japanese guard on a jungle path to make our way back to the camp we came from. A braver man than I might have thought about making an escape. It certainly did enter my head, but rapidly went out again.

We were both in urgent need of medical attention and felt it was going to take us a long time to walk three miles back at our own pace. We had no food, could not speak the language and knew that anyone sheltering us would be liable to be shot. No! " Survival was for me". My companion was with me in the decision. The first mile was uneventful, we neither saw nor heard anyone. As we neared the Japanese Army camp the road widened into a sort of clearing with the most direct road near the camp entrance where there was a sentry on duty. We decided to appear unconcerned and just staggered past as best we could and just looked at the sentry and would have stopped if he challenged us. He completely ignored us as if it was quite common for enemy POWs to stagger past his camp. When we were out of sight we sat down for a rest and to steady our nerves. We felt we must make it back to our camp before dusk at 6 o'clock as the Japs often travelled at night. We approached the next Jap camp with as much trepidation as we had the previous one. Again we met no-one on the forest path. We walked past this camp but there was no sentry on duty and we got out of sight as quickly as we could. Our own POW camp was just on the fringe of the jungle and we came on it suddenly and were spotted by the sentry and just walked back into the camp without question .

I thought perhaps our own Commandant may want us to lie low in the camp in case anyone had the chance to escape. We would then be able to stand in for them at Japanese roll calls. Our officers decided to report our return to the Japs and that was the last we heard of the incident.

I reported sick the next morning and was given a hot water foot bath with some Permanganate of Potash in and put on light duties in the camp instead of going to work on the railway.

CHAPTER NINE

TYASO CAMP

It would appear that I would probably remain at this camp for some time. Of this I was pleased in that most of my friends were with me here at Tyaso. After a few days the Japanese were demanding that every man should be available for work outside the camp. This meant that unless you were unable to stand you had to work outside. Up until this time there was no place in the camp where patients could be looked after in their own hut with medical staff.

About twenty men,including me, were taken to a site some quarter of a mile from the main camp and shown and area which was dense jungle. The Japanese guard said "You men build hut for 100 men as at other camp". We had about a dozen or so sharp 'Parangs' and a few cutting hooks for the undergrowth. We hacked away above ground disturbing snakes, ants, lizards and all manner of small animals. The first thing the guard did was to cut himself a bamboo pole and sharpen the end. This he used to prod or beat anyone who stopped work or seemed to be working too slowly. We just had short trousers and perhaps short socks and no protection against all manner of biting insects and sharp brambles. The bamboo was felled in long lengths and then trimmed off ready to be cut into appropriate lengths for the huts. Some of the creeper was kept to be used for tying for the sides and roof. Once we had a small area cleared we were given one chunkel or spade and holes were dug for the four corner posts and entrances at each end. The hut rapidly took shape and various poles were tied together with the creeper ready for the ready made fronds sewn together with more creeper to put on the roof and sides. The work was hard and the hours long and when we returned to camp the meal was a cupful of stew and rice and a cup of tea which was inadequate to keep us from starvation.

We were sleeping in huts with about a hundred men in each. Bamboo platforms built of split bamboo poles placed near together and tied with creeper were built about two feet from the floor. The space allowed was about two feet per man which men you slept with knees almost straight or on your back. If you got up in the night you were bound to disturb at least two people. By nine or ten at night most people were asleep. One night all was quiet when the Japs came round and roused everyone in the hut to fall in and make up a work party. It was very dark in the huts as there were no windows and the only light came in from the two entrances at either end. The getting dressed in the dark was no problem as most of us only had a pair of shorts and a khaki shirt and we slept in those anyway. Within five minutes we were outside and about sixty men were in the party with two Jap guards. We collected torches which appeared to be made from tightly bound rushes. The Japanese guards led us towards the river. We arrived at the river bank and were told to station ourselves at intervals where we could get a foot hold on the very steep sides of the river bank.

A barge was moored at the river side which was built entirely of bamboo poles fastened together with ties of creeper and even had a little hut in the center for the pilot. The actual barge was also the cargo and the "cargo" had been drifted and steered for miles down the river.

Four men had to get in the river and cut the bindings under the direction of the bargee, as if the wrong ties were cut in the wrong sequence, the whole thing could collapse and drift away down stream. The top layers of the vessel consisted of panels of fronds sewn with raffia ready made for the roof and sides of the huts. These were about two feet by about four feet. Each panel had to be passed from hand to hand up the steep bank of the river and then piled up for moving later. After the panels came the poles, and this was hazardous as the ends were razor sharp. It was two in the morning before we unloaded the last pole and were gathered together to be marched back to the camp.

The next day we went back to work as usual about 8.00 a.m. on the building site. Unfortunately, I was given a cross-cut saw and told to work with a guy who had never seen one before. This particular one was a real lumberjacks saw with big teeth and large handles. I tried to instruct my partner not to push the saw at any time, but to pull alternately with me, otherwise the saw buckled and the one pulling got nowhere. After a while we managed to get some sort of rythm going .

We were sawing tree trunks some three feet thick and the noise of the saw was the predominant noise on the site, so that every time we stopped working a Jap guard came across with a menacing bamboo pole which pursuaded us to get to work again. The resultant logs were split with wedges and fourteen pound hammers. In spite of our starvation diet we put on muscle weight whenever we were working on heavy manual work, and personally I think I felt better mentally but totally exhausted at the end of the day. Each night as we went back to our base, we carried as many logs as possible to use on the cooking fires. Everything to build the huts from the site was of natural growth and made without any metal, yet they would withstand very heavy tropical storms .

We had no motorised power to lift tree trunks or move earth, so the smaller straight branches were cut to a length to go underneath the large trunks and enough at each side for two men to get hold of the pole. There would be about twenty men holding the poles on each side of the tree trunk. In some cases we were made to move them before the side branches had even been cut off. The branches and leaves were covered by masses of red ants, and as you touched them, they would swarm over your body biting and leaving weals that were extremely painful .

I remember one instance when we were all in place to lift when the Jap guard gave the signal. There was a tremendous effort by all concerned, but the tree never moved. The guard shouted at us and then hit some of us with the bamboo stick which brought worse weals than the ants did. At the next signal to heave, the tree lifted off the ground and was carried forward to where it was needed. This was a classic example of wielding the big stick with effect.

There was not enough bamboo to construct all the huts needed. We were sent into the jungle in pairs with a parang each to cut down bamboo of at least ten foot lengths, and come back with at least twenty poles each. The guard was waiting to check that we had as many as he asked for and if anyone was short they had to go back and make the quantity up .

Many ruses were used to try to get away with less than the quota, such as putting some short ones at the end to the guard for counting. This was soon realised by the guards and no-one was allowed a break until the whole quota was brought in. After the midday break we were again sent out, but there was an odd number of men, so I had to go alone and bring in the twenty poles by myself. I was delighted but did not want to appear too keen. I went away into the bush with the others and then slipped away into a thicker part of the forest where I had seen a good clump of bamboo. I discovered quite a few ready cut poles and was able to collect enough in a short time.

I went into the bushes and lay down for a short rest as if I went back early they would have sent me back for a second load. The peace and the feeling of being alone for the first time in so long was exhilarating and for about half an hour I lay there listening to the cacophony of bird song, animal calls and the gentle flutter of leaves falling. I watched the ants crawling about over the ground and over my body. They only bite if you disturb them.

Suddenly from behind me the noise of an axe ripping into a tree broke the silence. I could hear voices, but the undergrowth was so thick that I didn't know how far away they were. The chopping went on ans I was very comfortable and was in no hurry to move. Now I realised the noises were replaced by what appeared to be warning shouts, and the creak of splitting timber. I looked skywards, and to my horror saw a huge tree falling in my direction. I panicked and tried to run through the undergrowth but caught my foot in a bramble and fell into the brush. I lay waiting for the crunch as I could see a large part of the tree falling around me. When it had settled, I moved my legs and was able to stand up to find myself surrounded by huge branches all round me and overhead, all of which had actually missed crushing any part of me. I said aloud "Thank you God" and thought that maybe there was someone up there looking after me.

I picked up my bundle of poles and made my way back to check them in with the guard.

A party of us were working near the railway when we were sent further along the line where an engine had been derailed. The engine was still upright, but all the wheels had come off the track.

These, by British standards, were huge wood burning giants and we had no machinery to help lift them. the task looked hopeless, but with the help of our manual jacks we lifted it a few inches and then with tree trunks as levers, pushed it off the jacks nearer to the rails. The rails were then taken off the sleepers and moving the engine about a foot at a time, we eventually had it in line with the rails. The one side was now leaning heavily to the other side and needed more power to right it. We sawed large timber blocks and rested the wheels in the middle on these whilst replacing the track under the front and back wheels. Another small lift and we could replace the centre track. It was amazing what could be done and the extra effort that was put into the whole operation under the threat of a beating. Forcing prisoners to do this was one way of discarding the sabotage of the lines which often happened .

On our way back to camp after this episode, we had to cross a very sandy cart track through the jungle. This was used by a team of yak carts driven by Indian drivers which were used to carry sleepers from the nearest railhead to make the new line that was to be built to link Singapore with Burma. As we came to the road we could see in the distance a cloud of dust and we heard shouting and the rattle of the carts. Out of the dust appeared three bullock carts each drawn by two bullocks, the front two were racing side by side and the third was whipping his beasts as hard as he could to try and pass the front ones. They were paid on the basis of how many sleepers they carried and were anxious to get back to load before darkness set in.

I understand there was alot of betting on the races and that was an added incentive. There were no motor wagons so far off the main roads and everything had to be carried by these carts or on the river. As the railway line progressed of course more and more steel rails and sleepers came up on the trains.

We were all getting more skilled in the operations involved in hut building and as they were for our own use, it was important to build them as quickly as possible and make them waterproof by putting the roof panels on carefully. I was in and around this camp for the next months building huts or making roads. Quite often we would be called out at midnight to unload a bamboo boat at the rivers edge. We only had torches made of twigs to light the area ans it was easy for some men to slip back into the camp unnoticed by the guards. The boats had to be unloaded so their absence meant those left had to work harder and longer.

One night we were left with only twenty men, when the Japs held a check before we went back to camp. They took the twenty left and marched us to their stores and gave us some cigarettes to divide amongst ourselves. There were three each and when we got back to the camp we told the others of our windfall. The value of cigarettes was equal to about three weeks pay. Those who had deserted and gone back to the camp were furious and wanted us to share the reward with them .

CHAPTER TEN

A PRIMITIVE EXISTENCE

Tyaso was a camp made by the Prisoners of War out of thickly afforested jungle, and the only man made tools we had were parangs (which were heavy curved knives used locally to chop wood), one hand saw, one large crosscut saw and a number of chunkels which are used as spades but are really large hoes. We had no wheeled transport of any kind. If trees had to be moved we did it by rolling, lifting on poles or stretcher like things made from bamboo. If we were moving soil we had baskets with woven handles. Any buckets were made by cutting down oil drums.

The river which ran near to the camp was a wide navigable river which flowed swiftly and rose, perhaps forty feet between its high banks in the monsoon rains.

A dirt track ran past the camp and two or three gangs of perhaps two or three hundred men, women and children were marched along here on their way to work on the railway. Most of these were Malayans or Tamils and many had difficulty in walking. They all carried their belongings on their heads. Many appeared ill and all were terribly thin. We at least were legitimate Prisoners of War, but it appeared these people had been forced to labour for the Japanese and had been picked up at random and transported to another country. A transit camp for these people was within sight from certain parts of our camp and every morning we could see men with a large grass mat stretched between two bamboo poles carrying their dead away to be buried.

Sometimes there were men under guard in front of a hut with

their hands bound behind their backs and a string tied to parts of their naked bodies with a stone on the ground between them so that if either of them moved if would be extremely painful to them.

We had no well within the camp and all water had to brought up from the rive and of course boiled before being used. The water for drinking was boiled in large metal cauldrons for which we constructed mud bases to lay them on and a space for the fire underneath. We were thus able to use fairly large pieces of wood to burn and thereby save some woodcutting. Ovens too were constructed of mud, but as we seldom had anything to bake other than rice cakes they were not of great use and were constructed more in hope than for immediate use.

We slept in long huts which I have already described and these gave us some problems.If you had to leave your bedspace during the dark nights, it was best to hang some sort of article infront of your space which you could feel for on your return. I went out one night and thought it was exceptionally dark and yet I had been up before on that night and it was moonlit. After groping my way out of the hut I realised I had failed to open my eyes.

The latrines were trenches dug in the forest and were some distance away from the huts. In the dark it was not unusual to stumble into a bullock which was invariably as scared as you were and would give a great bellow and go crashing away through the scrub. Fireflies were useful on the very dark nights.

When we were taken to unload the river boats or rafts, there was no landing stage and so we had to negotiate a narrow plank with sacks of rice in 100lb bags. We were weak from lack of food and every sack meant an enormous effort even to get it onto our backs and the walk across the plank was a nightmare to me as if we fell it would have been into the fast flowing water.

One night during the unloading of a bamboo raft the last twenty or so poles were anchored to the river bank and the men, who were working on the raft in the water, had left their clothes and boots on the bank. They made a mistake and untied the anchor rope and the remains of the raft went drifting down the river and disappeared out of site round a bend with three naked sailors. They arrived back in the camp the next morning with scratches in many places from the bush and undergrowth they'd had to battle through.

During one of our stints at the riverside, a larger than usual raft arrived and shortly afterwards a section of the Japanese Field Artillery came complete with six cannons similar to the ones which had forced us off the road earlier in our journey up country. We were ordered by the Japs to help them load these onto the raft. After a lot of protest from our Officer in Charge we reluctantly and under duress from bayonets agreed to help the loading. Planks were placed to take the wheels and ropes were attached to the cannon, we pulled at the wrong time and misunderstood all the Jap instructions so successfully that after we nearly succeeded in getting the cannon and the two Japs in the water and a lot of face slapping later, they decided they would be safer loading the guns themselves. They were very angry and we were glad to see them away up the river.

We had hardly settled at Tyaso when the rains started and the monsoon broke. Cholera had now claimed a few deaths and men were going down every night with symptoms. An isolation area was set up by the Japanese half a mile from the main camp. Volunteers were called for, to man the new area. The Japanese refused to go anywhere near cholera. Men of whom had no medical experience were picked from the volunteers and taking all their belongings with them, went cheerfully on a mission that was wholly humanitarian and extremely brave as their lives were in jeopardy for 24 hours a day.

We were seldom given the opportunity to get our hair cut and mine had got longer than I liked it to be. The reason was that anyone who had scissors coupled with a very slight knowledge of hair cutting was in great demand and could charge a high price.

A man who had recently come to live in our hut offered to cut mine after he had finished the man he was giving a short back and sides to. There was some banter over the result of the previous operation and someone said "Give him a close crew cut" as I sat in the barbers chair which was a sawn branch of a tree. Eventually after some argument I said "ok take the lot off, I may not need another then until we are free." He said "you are a bloody optimist, if you leave it that long it will be down to your waist."

Within ten minutes, the midges smelled new bare flesh and attacked in their hundreds and I spent the rest of the evening trying to protect my head. During that night the barber was taken ill with cholera and was taken away to the isolation area. He would have to be left some distance from the isolation area and then orderlies from the cholera area would come and take him in. The Japanese were terrified and would come nowhere near the affected hut. They ordered his kit that was left behind must be burnt and everyone must move out and the hut burnt down. The first night we slept out in the open, in spite of sleeping with my hat on, the sand flies tormented me all through the night.

When we came back from work in the evening, there was an old tent left for us to erect. It was one of those round ones which were used in the first world war and was in two parts the outer and an inner lining. As there were still some forty men wanting shelter, we erected the two parts as two separate tents. I had reported sick that morning but had been passed fit to work. We had to make the necessary tent pegs and by nine o'clock it was ready for occupation. In order to make room for us all, we slept heads and feet alternately toward the centre of the pole. During the night we had a tropical storm and the tent I was in was the fly part which was not waterproof. We were lying just on ground sheets and a blanket and the water was lapping round my ears when I awoke.

I stood up and immediately fell down again. I stood up again and found myself lying in the water. I realised I had a temperature and got up very slowly. My friends were full of sympathy and said if I could not eat my breakfast could they have it. I knew my life had been saved by my eating even when I had no desire for food. A blood sample proved I had malaria. I do not remember how I went to hospital which was a long hut over the other side of the camp. There was no room on the platforms, so I was put on the floor with the others who were just as ill as I was. There were no drugs or medicine available. The orderlies were overworked and apart from trying to get water for us and perhaps a little bit of marmite or a teaspoonful of condensed milk we had very little to eat.

I understand that I was there for three weeks altogether but apart from occasionally realising, but not caring where I was I do not remember the first two weeks. The third week I was conscious and realised I had not had a wash all the time I was there. Owing to the cholera which was supposed to be present in the water in the river, even water for washing had to be boiled. I managed to get down to the river by myself although staying on my feet and walking was difficult I was able to slide down the steep banking to the river. We were warned not to wash our faces or immerse in the water beyond our ribs because it was believed that the cholera was present in the surface of the water. I had taken a shirt and my shorts with me to wash, and believe me they needed washing after lying down in them for three weeks without a wash.

We did not have any soap or towels, these had worn out some time back, but if you beat your clothes on a rock it forced the dirt out and drying them in the hot sun cleaned and bleached. Feeling very clean and refreshed bodily, but my face and hair was still filthy, I began to clamber back up the river bank. The exertion was too much and I collapsed onto the muddy bank and had to crawl on hands and knees back to the hut. I was covered in mud and my washing was as dirty as ever. I crawled back into my bedspace and went to sleep. When I awoke, the mud had dried and the blanket was stuck to my body, however, the first steps to recovery had been taken and in another few days I was back at work again.

My first job was to fetch the stew from the cookhouse to the hut. It was some ten minutes walk. The buckets were carried on each end of a bamboo pole and the pole slung across the shoulders. The camp was a sea of mud and water and as I was barefoot I knew not what I would step on with each stride. The realisation was that if this stew was split, fifty men would be without a vital meal, its safe arrival was an enormous relief. One of my boots disintegrated and I had to go barefoot until I could find another right boot to go with the left one I still had. I was given a boot two sizes bigger than the one I had left, from a man who'd had his right leg amputated. The different weight of the footwear caused a limp until I got used to them.

There was now very little paper to be had in the camp and even bibles we being used for rolling cigarettes. Toilet paper was non-existent and the next best material were leaves. I found a tree which had really tough large leaves. I used to go in secret to pick them as everyone wanted them and I knew the tree would be stripped of all its leaves within reach if its location was disclosed.

We did not consider stealing from the Japs wrong, but getting caught was stupid. One of the men from our hut was caught stealing petrol to sell outside the wire. In addition to standing to attention for half a day at the guardhouse and being hit with a rifle butt whenever he relaxed, he was sentenced to kneel infront of our hut and the Japanese made everyone run past and slap him in the face. The hut had about a hundred men housed in it. If anyone was seen to be less than enthusiastic they were forced to join the queue at the back and hit him again .

CHAPTER ELEVEN

KANCHANBURI

I entered in my log book on September 4th 1943. "I am now back in a place called Kanchanburi after a spell of about four months living at Tyaso totally surrounded by trees and thick scrub. I have no need to write down the details, I shall forever remember them. It feels like being released from a very small cell. Where we were before was all thick jungle - but here there are open spaces, roads, a railway and herds of cows grazing in the clearings."

We were brought down from Tyaso in railway wagons normally used for the transport of sacks of rice.1 The sun made the metal sides unbearably hot during the day and cold at night when the sun had set. The conditions in the trucks were even worse than on the journey up country as about 70% of the men had either dysentry, Beri-Beri, ulcers on the legs, malaria or just starvation. By the time we arrived at Kanchanburi four of our passengers had died.

At the front of the train were two truckers with girls from the Japanese brothel at Tyaso who, I presume, were going on leave. We stopped beside a hutted camp and after a long delay whilst the guards tried to account for all their cargo of human misery, orderlies came from the camp and helped us get down from the high trucks. There were so many who were not able to walk that the stretcher bearers had to make many return journeys before the last man was behind the perimeter fence.

The smell of rotting flesh from the ulcers, the primitive sanitation and the filthy state of the inmates was unbelievable even to us who were hardened to such degradation.

The latrines were long open huts with an attap roof and bamboo poles to stand on over a trench dug underneath. When the rains came they filled with water so we dug new ones on higher ground and covered the old ones with grass matting and then a layer of soil on top. More rains came and one end of our hut was under water to only three of four inches under the bedspace. We had to walk through water up to our knees to get to our beds.

One or two train loads of sick men began to arrive from the railway camps up country every week. They mostly arrived at night and the Japs would come round the huts and every man who could walk was sent to help unload the men on it. Almost every train had dead bodies aboard and in some cases had buried men in the jungle on the way down. We had a limited number of stretchers and after helping those who could stagger along to their allotted bed spaces, we had to make journeys for the stretcher cases. Each stretcher needed two men at each end as we were too weak to carry a man and his gear.

We found one man in a corner of one truck and he was moaning and groaning and appeared quite helpless and it was with alot of struggling and lifting we managed to get him on the stretcher. He appeared to be dying so we asked an orderly if he could do anything for him and left to bring more cases in. During all the time we were unloading this train the water was about eighteen inches deep and we were staggering along in bare feet no knowing where to tread. I was also conscious that we were passing near where the latrines had been, and if we stepped over them they would give way and we would be in trouble. One patient complained we were splashing him as we struggled through the water. Some gratitude! We were all exhausted by now and were glad to get the last man off the train and settled in a hut.

I had a few minutes to spare before morning roll call and went to see the man with all the luggage who appeared to be dying to see if there was anything I could do for him. His bed was empty and I asked the orderly if he had died. "No" he said "he's around here somewhere". As I was leaving the hut I met him carrying some cigarettes and a spare pair of shorts, and he said he had been trying to sell them in another hut. I told him what I thought of him. Whilst we had been struggling with him we could have helped a more deserving case. This type, thank goodness, were in the minority.

More and more very sick men were coming down on the trains particularly with very bad leg ulcers. One day I had been with a party to get wood from the forest and was carrying the only saw in the camp. A man from the hospital met us and asked for the saw as they had an amputation to do back at the camp. Ours was the only suitable saw .

There was no operating theatre as such, but a bench constructed from bamboo poles with a split bamboo top substituted for an operating table. This was placed in the space between two huts. The patient was laid on this bench and in some cases knocked unconscious, because anesthetics were not always available. At each corner of the bench was an orderly with a fly swot and someone else held a mosquito net to try and keep the hordes of blood smelling insects at bay.

The doctors worked long hours under appalling conditions and without the necessary bandages and dressings. To them it must have been very frustrating, knowing what they could have done had they had the instruments, facilities and drugs normally available to them.

The single line railroad that passed by the camp was sometimes used by repair gangs travelling on a man propelled maintenance truck. One morning a dog was hit and killed by one of these trucks and the body was left at the lineside. Within five minutes some vultures swooped down and with the King Vulture perched on a stump at the line side the others stripped all the flesh off it in ten minutes and were back up in the sky ready to spot the next casualty.

I occasionally went out with a work party and two Japanese guards with a truck to collect firewood for the cookhouse. People who had timber fo r sale stacked the timber between stakes driven into the ground at metre intervals and filled to a metre high and sold at so much per square metre. It was great to get out of the camp and drive along the roads to see the countryside from the trucks. As some of these were off the main road in the forest we often got bogged down.

The Japs got so excited and revved up the engines until the wheels were in as deep as the axles. They refused to take our advice on principal, but when all their efforts had been in vain and the truck was well and truly stuck they would go some distance away for a smoke. We would rest for a while and then with logs and large piece of timber for levers and props we never failed to get the truck free in good time to finish work at the usual time.

On another of these expeditions we went into a small town and the Japanese allowed us to go into a Cafe with them. We were allowed to buy one cup of tea, but we had no more money to buy food .

When I was first detailed for one of two Burial Squads the Cemetery was bout half a mile away from the camp. It then contained some twenty graves. We were given two pick axes and a chunkel. An area of about 50 square yards had been cleared of trees and some of the scrub, but many of the tree roots were still in the ground. The ground was reasonably soft for about a foot deep, but after that it was all pick and shovel work. The sun beat down on us and it was not always possible to have our water bottles filled before setting out.

The bodies of those dying during the night were put outside the huts and our first task was to count them and pick up our first body and load it onto the stretcher. We had to travel out of the camp and then about a hundred yards down the road, across a ditch and onto a winding jungle path with overhanging branches. The stretchers were made with two ten foot bamboo poles which were pushed through the corners of two rice sacks. These were very unstable and needed every effort to prevent the body falling off the stretcher.

Altogether the two grave digging squads preparing the graves and four or five men bringing the bodies from the camp would be burying as many bodies as twenty per day. Some bodies were bloated by Beri-Beri to twice their normal weight, other weighed as little as five stones. Sometimes you would recognise a friend whom you did not know was in the camp. It was an awful job but had to be done and was done as reverently as the circumstances permitted.

When digging one grave, we came upon an old human skull but no other bones were with it. We showed it to the Japanese guards and asked if we could re-bury it somewhere. They took it off us and played football with it before throwing it into the thick scrub.

From pictures now being published this same place is a place of pilgrimage for relatives and friends of those who are buried there. It is beautifully kept by the War Graves Commission.

Water was very scarce in this camp and we only got a wash every two or three days. If you could find a bucket and manage to get to the well and join the queue and bring back some water, you would be besieged by all your friends and a few more to use the remains of the dirty water after you had finished it. No water was thrown away, someone would pour the very last drop onto their body.

We had not seen soap for nearly a year and very few men had any sort of cloth to use as a towel. We really were filthy and what clothes we had were saturated each day by sweat. The ration of rice allowed by the Japanese was continually being cut down, and more and more men were dying from starvation. The sick were intermingled with the not so sick which meant that disease was spreading rapidly.

A plague of lice started at one end of the hut. It gradually crept from one man to the next. I sat on my bed watching men sat with their trousers on their knees picking lice from the seams and crushing them one by one. It was a hopeless task, and eventually everyone in the hut was lousy. This caused more skin scratching. My main worry was always that I would develop leg ulcers which just ate away the flesh until the leg had to be amputated. the smell from these ulcers was horrible and was with us day and night.

A new camp had been built in another part of Kanchunabri as a hospital camp to receive some of the very sick coming down from the Burma railway. I was in a detail of about 100 men to go to this new camp and help to get it ready for a large contingent of very sick and wounded men expected within a few weeks.

Although we were amongst men available to move, most of us were suffering the after effects of dysentery, malaria, denge fever, leg ulcers and cholera. We were marched the few miles from our previous camp near the railway. I say march, which implies an orderly body of men proceeding along in some order, but the better description was, we staggered along with the aid of sticks and in some cases stretchers.

As soon as we had passed the Japanese guard hut at the new camp three of us broke away from the main body of men and went in search of a quiet tent, hut or bush where we would be, perhaps, less conspicuous and therefore less likely to be called on for duties. We found a small tent all ready pitched and the floor seemed reasonably dry and clean. We realised being in a tent would mean we would have to sleep on the floor, but it was an earth floor and therefore not as hard as concrete .

The huts would have attap benching about two feet from the ground and were much softer and less plagued by ants and other insects. We had spent many nights on concrete floors with only blankets to soften the hardness.

Since we were prisoners, I remember sleeping for about a week on solid concrete and found a wooden door with panels on it and it was unbelievable to find that the greater comfort of the softness of the door was almost like a straw mattress. Our vision of a little peace and quietness in our new found "home" was soon rudely shattered by the Sergeant poking his head through the tent flap and demanding "The Nips want two men to go to the Japanese Commandants quarters. I have got one, and you Wilson, are the other one." My two friends said they would try and keep a place for me in the small tent when I came back .

CHAPTER TWELVE

NO CHANCES WASTED

No-one liked working directly with the Japs, but orders were orders and I was determined not to break my rule of not dodging any task in case the alternative was worse.

There was a young Australian waiting outside the tent and he was to be my workmate on the job. The Sergeant took us to the Japanese lines and handed us over to two young Japanese guards. Neither of them could speak English, nor could we speak Japanese. However, they eventually got me to understand that we would have to fetch food from the cookhouse for the two guards and whatever Officers were around at the time. We would also have to fetch water from the well which was about half a mile away.

There were three huts surrounding a small square of sandy earth. One of these, from where we would be working, consisted of an open ended attap hut with a wood table which was the dining table for the Ordinary Soldiers, and opposite was the Officers "House". The furnishing was very sparse and consisted of a collapsible Army bed and a table about eighteen inches high with a hole in the middle. Under the hole there was a paraffin heater on which they put the food to keep it hot during a meal.

Our first job was to serve coffee. Underneath the table an ex-British Army Hay Box which was used normally to keep food hot for up to eight hours. They had put ice (bought in the local town) in the bottom part and a bowl of coffee in the top and we served them iced coffee .

A fire burnt underneath a large iron pan which was suspended from crossed bamboo poles by a piece of wire. It was already boiling. Aussie got out the mugs and we were shown where they kept the sugar and tea. He had the good sense to put out five mugs, three for them and two for us! We intended to play the opportunities right from the beginning. I ladled the boiling water into the mugs and no remarks were made by the Japs. We stood with our backs to them whilst putting in the sugar and took care to put about three spoonsful in our coffee. We had not tasted sugar for nearly two years and it sure was nectar .

At this stage only a few words had been spoken amongst us. We were told to go and fetch our kit from the tent and one of the guards would show us where we would be sleeping. We were taken to a long hut at the far end of the camp which was divided by attap panels across the middle. One half contained all the rations for both the Japanese and the British and the other half had straw mats about a foot off the floor resting on bamboo frames for our sleeping quarters. This housed all the POW's who were working in the kitchen and ourselves.

Opposite this hut was the cookhouse itself and we were taken to the Japanese cook who was told that we were to be given anything we asked for, for the Shoko. He gave us a nasty look and grunted. Here, I thought was a problem to be overcome carefully. This proved to be right .

The Japanese Officers quarters where we were to work were surrounded on two sides by fairly thick jungle within the wire surrounds of the whole camp. We arranged to get our meals direct from our own cookhouse as we could not always get away at ordinary meal times. This meant we had an excuse to have our mess tins with us at the Nips hut in case we needed them to hide some coffee, sugar or anything else that was portable and eatable.

So began a more interesting and challenging period in my captivity. I was able to do things and make decisions myself and bear the consequences of those decisions. I was able to do things for myself and if I got into trouble with the guards, it was up to me to get out of it myself without the whole camp suffering.

Occasionally, we were detailed to go with a party to bring in the daily rations for the whole camp. The Japanese Quarter Master bargained with the local traders and then we loaded his purchases on to the wagon under very close scrutiny of the guards incase we pinched anything. When we got the stuff back to the camp and unloaded it, we were briefed by our own cooks to stack the foodstuff against the partition between the stores and our living quarters. Eggs were in large wicker baskets and were eighteen inches deep in each basket. In spite of this they were seldom broken. As we unloaded each basket it was put right against the attap fence and we marked where it was by tearing a frond and pushing it through the gap to mark the position on the other side of the partition. Later if the Japanese guards who lived in the stores were out, we could reach through the gap and take eggs out of the baskets. The same procedure was done for sweet potatoes. The rice sacks had to be slit with a penknife and the rice caught in a mess-tin. The difficulty with rice was to find somewhere to cook it without being seen. There was no such problem with the eggs, we bit the tops off and sucked the contents out and then carefully disposed of the shells.

One evening three Japanese Officers from another camp arrived unexpectedly. Our Shoko instructed us to get eight eggs from the cookhouse and fry them for his guests. As is was late I had to find the Japanese Head Cook and get permission to get the eggs from the store. He cursed and grumbled about my disturbing him at night and said I could not have any eggs. I said to him "ok I'll tell Shoko you give me no tomargos (eggs) for his Shoko friends." He told me to go and get the tomargos from the store and waited outside whilst I collected them. I went to the basket in the store and put eight eggs into my mess tin, had a look round and saw that he was no looking my way and slipped another two eggs into each pocket in my shorts. As I came out of the hut I showed him that I only had eight eggs in the tin. He muttered all sorts of threats and curses but dare no hit me in case I told the Shoko .

Gordon, the Australian who worked with me, met me half way back from the stores to say that the visitors were not staying and he had been sent to cancel the order. There was no way we were going to give the eggs back to the cook. We both had shirts on so Gordon put four down his shirt and the other four in his two trouser pockets and took them back to our sleeping quarters. That left me with two in each trouser pocket and an empty mess tin to show that I had not collected the eggs .

I was suprised to see Wakabioshi (the Jap Commander) sitting at the table where we worked, as he normally never came to us at night. "I have cup of coffee" he said. There were wooden forms at either side of the table and the coffee was in an icebox under the table, and the three Japs were sat on the forms. How was I going to bend down and reach for the box and get the bottle of coffee out without breaking the eggs in my pockets? I knelt down and managed to open the top and extract the bottle of coffee but as I straightened up I felt a slow trickle of egg down one leg. However, it was dark so no-one noticed and I was able to pour the coffee and sit down on the form until the party broke up.

I made my way back to our sleeping quarters and we had eleven eggs to divide. We managed to wake two of our friends and told them to bring their mugs to our bed space. We broke them into the mugs and beat them up with a fork and drank them raw. What a feast we had and they tasted better for having been stolen from the Japs .

Two or three nights later Wakibioshi decided to have a party in his hut. We had another Japanese Officer living in the hut attached to the area we served the meals in. When he came to the camp he brought with him a large glass Carboy filled with red liquid. I often wondered what was in it. Two other Japanese Officers arrived. In Wakibioshi's hut there was an oval table about a foot high with a round hole in the middle, and underneath they put a Primus Stove and cooked some steaks and various vegetable in an oval dish. The guests squatted on the floor and used the chopsticks to keep picking the food straight from the cooking dish .

The Officer from our mess came over and told me to fill a kettle, which he produced, with drink from the Carboy and fill three bottles, which he also provided, with the contents which turned out to be Port Wine. He left me to fill the bottles from the kettle and went back to the party. When we had filled them, there was still some left in the kettle. This we poured into our mess tins and hid them away. Shortly afterwards the Main Gate Guard turned up with three girls and took them into the Officers Hut. We presumed they were from the local brothel which the Japanese had set up in the nearest town. We kept being called over to the party and given the bottles to refill and each time we had half a mug of wine left over, which we swallowed with relish .

By eleven o'clock (estimated time as no POW still had a watch at this stage, they had all been sold for money to buy food from over the wire) the wine was working and the party was going merrily with singing, the piano was being thumped and rather maudlin laughter coming from the Shogos hut. Aussie and I seemed as if we may be drunk for the first time for nearly three years and the situation was getting dangerous. The revellers would have to pass close to our huts on their way to the camp exit. They would not be loathe to a round of POW baiting as they had swords with them we did not want to encounter them at close quarters.

We waited in the shadow of our hut for the guests to leave. The first to come out of the Shogos hut was the smallest of the guests. He managed to get as far as the path past our hut, without falling down but as he passed us the sword belt was not very tight and the scabbard got between his legs and over he went. We had to retreat further into the darkness as we were exploding with laughter at his antics to regain an upright position and as he faded into the darkness he was holding the sword in its scabbard by the bottom and staggering out of sight .

All had gone quiet at the party so we too staggered back to our hut hoping th guard wouldn't see us. I do not know what time the girls left, but the two Officers from our camp look rough the next morning .

Near the main gate but within the camp there was a large mango tree which had a fair crop on it, but even the lowest branches were at least ten feet from the ground. This was in sight of the main gate guardroom. Any prisoner caught trying to climb a tree was liable to be shot at and it was not worth it for a mango. Occasionally a ripe one would fall onto the ground, and if you happened to be near enough to grab it you were lucky. Sometimes very unripe ones were loosened by birds of monkeys and I managed to pick up a few on my way to the cookhouse. If you tried to eat an unripe one and the juice fell onto your skin, it would leave a painful acid burn which would take a few days to heal. I therefore kept the unripe one hidden until they were ripe .

Wakibioshi decided he would like some and keep them to ripen. Operation "Get the Mangoes" was put into action. A truck was brought to be stationed under the tree. The longest bamboo pole was found and a wire loop fastened to the sharp end. The Jap Officer mounted the truck and proceeded to lasso the ripest mangos he could see. He had some of the Jap guards running around to catch them as they fall. We were not asked to join in. It may have been that there would have been doubts about the probability of the falling mangos getting mislaid! Wakibioshi came back to the hut with two small baskets full of fruit. From somewhere he got a cardboard box, (something I had not seen for nearly a year) which was deep enough to store two layers of mangos. Into this I was told to put some dried grass from the scrub, and sort out the least ripe fruit and place them in the bottom. I was then given some sawdust to cover the bottom layer and the same for the next layer. "You put box and mangos in dark place" he said, "soon all mangos very juicy".

It was suggested that a good place to store them in was in the rafters of our hut with some dried fronds covering them. The riper ones he took away to eat. I had to stand on the table to get the box on the ledge. A few days later I was asked to get them down and see if any had ripened. They were still rock hard and so we were told to put them back in the dark. A few days later all was quiet and the Japs were away. Aussie and I decided to see if the Mangos were ripe. Two on the top layer were turning and would be ready to eat in a day or so. We took those two out and the thought came to us both at once. We took two unripe ones from our secret hoard and put them in the box and returned it to its dark place.

The next day Wakibioshi asked to see if any had ripened yet. There were two he thought ready. He took them and before the box was returned to its place in the roof, we replaced some of his riper ones with our very green ones. This happened a number of times, but eventually we ran out of replacements so we let him have the rest.

There had been trouble at a neighbouring camp over the possession of a radio by a prisoner resulting in the execution of a prisoner for refusing to reveal the whereabouts of any radio or components. Shortly after this event the Kempi (Secret Police) visited the camp and called for the British Office in Charge to be brought before him. We were on duty at the Japanese quarters when the Officer was being questioned in the hut opposite where we were, and as the interrogation went on we could see over the top of the hut wall exactly what was happening.

There was a lot of shouting and voices raised in anger by the

Japanese Kempi Officer. There were only the two men in the hut and eventually the Kempi produced a baseball bat and beat the British Officer over the head with it. This went on for what seemed to us a long time but eventually our Officer was allowed to go back to his quarters with weals and swellings round his head and face.

The Kempi Officer then came across to our kitchen and calmly asked, with a pronounced American drawl, for a cup of coffee. We were very apprehensive as to what would happen next, but he ignored us and talked to the Korean Guards, finishing his coffee he walked out. We were very glad to see him go but expected him back anytime. The guards told us afterwards when we questioned them about the American accent that this man had spent three years at Harvard University before the war when he lived in America. He was about six foot tall, dark haired and was immaculately dressed in a white suit and collar and tie with white suede shoes. At no time during the grilling was our Japanese Commandant present. He was known to the Japs as "Yank". We were also told that these men have only the rank of Sergeant but no Officer in the Japanese Army can challenge what they do or how they behave whilst in their camps. I was glad to see him away and hoped for no further visits .

Because our sleeping quarters were at the end of the ration hut, the rice and other eatables began to attract rats and so they became a problem to us. We never saw them by day, but at night they would climb the bamboo on to our bed spaces and jump on us. The first man to realise in the dark what was attacking him would kick out under his blanket thus throwing the rat further down the bed space and causing Pandemonium throughout the hut until the rats bolted out at the far end .

After rats had also attacked the guards in the ration hut itself, they decided to do something about the menace. A working party was brought up to dig a trench all the way round the hut so that the rats would fall in. The odd thing was that although the trench was about four feet deep, I never saw a rat in it, but they ceased to bother us for which we were grateful.

After the trench was dug, we had a new man come to work in the cookhouse and therefore live in our hut. He was very quiet and never spoke, only to answer questions. He was allocated the bed space next to mine. This man had no mosquito nets but just before he got under his blanket he tied a Joss stick in the form of a Katherine Wheel with a piece of string to a bamboo beam of the hut. The smell of the burning stick was quite pleasant.

Later in the night I was awakened by his movement and realised there was an awful smell of burning wool and he was frantically beating out a small fire on his bed space and then tossed the smouldering blanket into the trench round the hut. I watched this but he handled the situation without disturbing anyone else and the danger appeared to be over. I went back to sleep and next morning thought "was there a fire last night or was I dreaming?" I looked down into the trench and sure enough there were the ashes of a blanket. It turned out he had used an ordinary piece of string to tie to the Joss stick and as it burnt round to where the string touched it, the stick itself fell onto his blanket and set it smouldering. The stupid guy had not realised that the way that the Thai's hung them up was with a piece of wire or put them on a plate to burn.

We had with us in the hut an Australian Army man who was working in the cookhouse with the Jap cooks. He was a known dealer in watches, rings, gold cigarette cases or any commodity the Thai's would buy on the black market. He was a likeable rogue but was always ready to do a good turn for his mates when he could.

Some of the Japs that worked in the cookhouse also did their turn on perimeter guard duty. He arranged to go out of the compound with one of the guards and visit a village to sell some things he and the Jap had bought from the prisoners. The compound was surrounded by a clearing about ten yards wide and in a straight line so that the guards had a clear view from the corner of two sides of the compound, another guard could cover for the other two sides. The two of them were challenged as they crossed the clearing and they both ran for cover. The Aussie fled to his bed space in our hut and quickly got under the blanket and feigned sleep. The rest of us also feigned sleep although the scuffle had awakened us all. Most of us spent the night in fear that he would be traced to our hut. We would have all been in dire trouble if he had been traced and they would probably beaten us all up for the offence .

There was a much more serious incident occurred at this time. One of our Medical Orderlies had been apprehended as he tried to cross the perimeter clearing and was found to be in possession of anti-malarial tablets and other medical drugs. These belonged to our stores and were very precious in view of the fact that any medicine was almost unobtainable .

The Japanese had never issued any drugs or medicines to us since our surrender and all we had left were from what we had brought into the camps from our own stores. They were now, after almost two years, very very scarce. He was on his way to a local village to sell them or exchange them for food or cigarettes. This could also give the Japanese the opportunity to say that if they gave us medicines we could sell them to the natives. This offence would normally have been dealt with by the Japanese. The punishment would probably have been to beat him and try and find out to whom he had been selling the Medicines. They would probably stand him outside the guardhouse and make him stand to attention there for most of the day. Any movement would result in the guard coming out of the guard room and beating the prisoner with a rifle butt. This often resulted in broken arms or ribs and facial injuries. As the sun moved round, the prisoner would be moved so as to keep him in the hot sun all the time. This caused dehydration and legs would often swell to twice normal size.

Wakibioshi, the camp commandant, decided in this case, perhaps because the offence was against our rules, and we the prisoners should be the ones to lose from this offence, to hand him over to the British camp commandant for punishment. He appeared before the British commandant and was found guilty of stealing drugs from the medical stores belonging to the POW's. The sentence was that he be paraded before the roll call parade in the evening which was the parade held every evening when the Japanese took a full count of all prisoners in the camp.

After the Japanese had dismissed their official parade the men were told to stand firm. The sentence was read out. It was that the offender be given a number of lashes with a bamboo cane in his bare back .

I was told by our sergeant to attend the parade but the rumour had gone around that this beating was going to take place. I was very much against the sentence and asked my Jap Officer if I could go, hoping he would say NO. As we were always needed for the Japanese meal around that time and I had not attended a parade since I had worked with the Japs I took a chance and went into the bush and found a place where I could see the Parade ground but could not be seen. All went normally until the handing over of the parade by the Japanese to the British Officer.

The senior British officer brought the parade to attention and produced the cane. He handed it to the next senior officer for him to administer the punishment. Absolute silence descended over the scene as the officer held the bamboo and after what appeared a long time to all those around, he slowly moved over to the next Officer and he accepted it but just stood still. There was further hesitation. Still a deathly hush was over the whole scene. There was a slight shuffle as one of the N.C.O.'s took a step forward turned smartly and walked away from the parade. This was followed by more and more men turning and dismissing themselves until the whole parade except the Officers and the prisoner and escort were left.

This was to me the nearest thing to mutiny that I had seen since joining the Army. It was not that anyone disagreed with the sentence of flogging but that the British soldiers should not be seen to uphold violence in their punishment of their own men. As far as most men were concerned, if the guilty man had been shot, that would have been fair punishment under different circumstances. To however, beat our own man in front of the Japanese guards, whilst we were complaining about the beatings, we were receiving from the Japanese did not make sense and they protested in the only way open to them.

The prisoner was eventually sentenced to be detained within the camp. He was made to do compulsory drill with loaded back packs every night on the parade square for 14 days.

After this incident of the mutiny, the British Camp Officer made it known that as punishment for insubordination the weekly bathing trip to the river was cancelled until further notice. I found out the Japanese guards were going to the river as usual on Thursday. I asked if one of us could go with them to the river and bring back some water for washing. Wakibioshi grinned and said, "you ask your Officer. He stop you going, not me. He run this camp now not me."

After a week the weekly bathing trip was restored. There was still little chance of having a wash unless you could get on the bathing party. To get fully immersed in the river was a real treat and helped to get rid of body lice and scabies.

Many of the men in this camp were very ill and wasted, and had suffered terribly working on the Burma railway. These trips to the river were a concession that was greater than any we had been granted since we were captured. To get away from the site and smell of the rotting flesh that hung over the whole area both night and day was a luxury in itself.

Those who were not fit to go to the river had some incentive to get well enough to walk the two miles or so through the rough jungle to the river. The part of the river they took us to had wide sandy beach like banks, and the water flowed at either side of an island in the centre. We stripped off on the banks as near to the water as we could, and first washed all the clothes we possessed, and then spread them out on the bank and put stones on them in case a breeze blew up and to help recognise your own pile. As we came out of the water the stones were so hot that you had to try and avoid treading on them.

Although I was still plagued with dysentery, I knew if I went on sick parade the Japanese would want to know from what I was suffering. Had I been working in our kitchen and handling our food, I would have been asked to be put on some task away from the chance of contaminating our food. I had no compunction about spreading infection amongst the Japs, but I knew they were terrified of any infectious diseases, and I would have been booted quickly out of sight.

I was still not much more than a skeleton and weighed around eight stone. My normal weight was twelve and a half stone. The extra bits of food I was getting from the Japs leftovers was keeping me on the level without losing more weight.

Behind the hut we worked in was scrubland and trees. This gave me the chance to go in there without going to the latrines in the camp. On one excursion, I came across a tomato plant on an old rubbish tip. This was covered with tomatoes about as big as a marble but red ripe. I went back to the hut to get my pint pot and quickly filled it with the fruit. I could have eaten them all at once, but I knew my stomach was in no state to accept such a lot of food at once. I ate some and Aussie and I shared the rest when we got back to our own hut. I had all sorts of offers of money from the men in the hut to show me where the plants were. Survival was far more use to me than money.

I was alone sat on a form in the open kitchen end of the Japanese hut. It was early afternoon, the Jap Officers and their Toebangs (batmen) were away. Aussie had gone to the river. The very fact of being alone was enjoyable as the only other time one could feel alone was if you woke up in the night and everyone except yourself was asleep.

The first thought was to rob the coffee and sugar tins and hide that away. I took a stroll round the Japanese Officers huts but the only thing I found was a Synoan Times printed in English underneath one of the huts. I stuck it down my shirt and looked forward to having something to read that night back at the hut.

Normally we spent all our time in shorts of a G-String, but if you were likely to come across something that was useful or eatable we always wore a shirt. I hid the paper away and sat down at the table under the shade of the hut roof. I was listening and enjoying the songs of the birds and the insects and the crack of the bamboo in the hot sun. I just stared at nothing in particular towards the far side of the open square I was facing.

I saw the undergrowth move on the far side of the open space. Quite slowly there appeared close to the ground, the head of a snake. I was fascinated as it leisurely slid across the clearing towards me. It did not appear to have seen me. I thought what a beautiful creature it was and it raised its head to be four or five feet high. I froze so not to frighten it away. Perhaps for thirty seconds it stared me straight in the eye. I also suddenly thought these things can be dangerous. Our eyes were on the same level and there was some six yards between us. It turned and slithered away into the bush. I followed it cautiously, but all trace of the creature had gone. I considered this was an encounter neither of us had won. I had encountered many snakes in Tyaso but never one this size before.

The Japanese occasionally came back into camp with a couple of chickens. I never knew whether they had just picked them up at the nearest Kampong, or if they had been legitimately bought. Their necks had been wrung. We plucked and gutted them before cutting the meat off the bones and slicing it into small squares. This meat was then put into an oval pan and cooked in some fat which the Japs provided. The rice would be cooked in the camp cookhouse along with their normal meal. It was usually laced with chilli or garlic. Unfortunately, we were within sight of some Japanese all the way from the cookhouse so we were unable to get our hands into the bucket to help ourselves. The rice was put into bowls and the chicken carried into their hut and placed in a mess tin on the Primus stove in the middle of their table. They sat round the table on the floor and picked up a piece of chicken with the chop sticks and then picked up some rice to go with it. Thus the chicken was always hot as it was eaten.

We left as much meat on the bones as we dare and put them into our mess tins and boiled them up over the fire. This soup was put on one side until we went back to our own hut or if it was late we took it straight to our friends who were most in need of it in the hospital beds. It there was anything left on the Jap plates we always ate it. If they had yak meat there may be lumps of gristle left on the plates and when it came to washing up time, we would take this and chew it for half an hour until no flavour or juice was left.

One of the Jap guard complained to the Japanese Commandant that we had been seen taking food over to the hospital huts in our mess tins. We had been quite open about this as it was only waste from the Japs point of view. The two Tobangs (batmen) with whom we worked did not mind us taking the waste away, so it was probably some of the other guards who could be very nasty. The outcome was we were told that we must not take anything away with us when we finished work at night. Normally we would be wearing our shirts after dark as some slight protection from mosquito bites and malaria. The answer was to carry our shirts underneath our arm having first wrapped it round a mess tin with whatever we could pinch concealed in it. No problem .

The two Tobangs (batmen) we were working with were reasonable and after a few weeks I managed a conversation in Pigdin English with them. One was a Korean school teacher in civilian life and had been conscripted into the Japanese Army. I got the impression when I talked alone with him, that he was a very reluctant conscript and had little respect for the Japanese. The other was very reserved and hardly ever spoke to us. He was not however, unpleasant.

Occasionally some of the ordinary guards came to visit. In some cases all they came for was to try and pick a quarrel with us. I found the best way to handle them was to either not understand them or to misunderstand and give a silly answer to their baiting us. I thought it better to appear stupid than to risk a beating up for no reason but pride .

Wokibioshi the Jap Shoko and Camp Commandant sometime came over to talk to us whilst we got his coffee ready. He occasionally relaxed and sat at our table. I remember one occasion when I was alone and he came over and I made his coffee and he sat at the table. He spilled some coffee on the table, dipped his index finger in it, and made a mark on the table top and said, "here Japanese troops" and the indicating in the same way "here Imphal" and left a mark infront of the Japanese Troops. Then at the other side of Imphal and said "bang! bang! bang!. Many killed both sides. No good. Very sad". He also told me on this occasion that he had two sons at school and one was a very keen baseball player. He also said that he had a furniture shop in Osaki.

Only once did he actually give us anything. One morning, he called us both over to his hut and said it was his birthday and gave us one cigarette each. There was no-one else about at the time and it appeared he did not want anyone else to know that he'd given us something. I think he knew some of the dodges we used to get spare coffee, eggs and rice. I was grateful that he could turn a blind eye to our thieving. Under any of the other camp Commandants, we would have been beaten up for every offence.

There was one event that may have been forbidden in any other camp. An old small portable church organ had come into the camp probably at the same time as the piano arrived. These were brought up with us to Bam Pong on the train and now reappeared at Kanchunaburi. It so happened that a young man named Williams was in this camp. He played the organ in civilian life and it was arranged he should give a concert in one of the hospital huts. The organ was carried to the hut and although it was on casters, they sank in to the earth floor we managed to find a fairly hard stand for it. We did not have a chair, so he sat on the bamboo staging which was our beds.

Someone provided a glass pint pot and half filled it with tea. This looked like ale and it was ledged on the top of the organ. The sound he got out of the organ was terrific. All those who could walk gathered around and he played all the hits which were current just before we left home. The pint pot rocked as the "beer" swilled around. all those who were well enough to speak, sang and even those who were unconscious seemed to revive a little.

The Japanese guard came into the hut to see what all the noise was about but after a short time left us alone. When he had gone we sang "Land of Hope and Glory" and "There Will Always be England" and other patriotic songs which were normally forbidden. I for one went to bed feeling much better than I had before the concert.

The Tobangs sometimes came in with hen and duck eggs to have with their rice. They bought these in the local kampongs. The Shoko's too sometimes brought eggs in to be boiled or fried. I think some of these eggs turned out to be bad. Wokibioshi came to me one day and said "I buy chickens. You build house for them." "O.K. how many" I replied. He held up six fingers and promised to get some attap panels and some bamboo poles for us to make a pen.

The next day we found a suitable site which I took care was out of site of any of the huts and we were given a hammer, a parang to clear the bushes and a chunkel to dig some holes for the posts. My mind boggled at the prospects looming before my vision. How about a pig. I could almost smell bacon and eggs every morning for breakfast. The attap panels and posts were brought in the next day by an Indian with a yak cart. Aussie and I soon had a pen built with a small hut for shelter and two perches and a small door to close at night. The Shoko gave the pen the thumbs up. He went off with the two Tobangs down to the Kampong and they came back with the chickens in a sack. We took them to the pen and released them.

I had never seen six scruffier chickens at once in my life before. They had hardly any feathers and very scaly legs. I would say none of them were under three years old. Shoko said "How soon we get tomargoes (eggs)" I picked one of them up and examined it as if I knew all about chickens. "About two weeks. Not old enough to lay yet" I said with as much conviction as I could. He had also bought some grain. It was unfortunately not all barley or wheat and there were some grains in it that I did not recognise. Otherwise we could all have had porridge for breakfast.

Actually they looked like old hens, but what I had in mind was that it would be a week or two before he would expect the first eggs. After about ten days we found the first egg. We hid it near the pen so that we could pick it up in the evening. Wakibioshi starting asking each day "Any tomargoes" and we would reply "Perhaps tomorrow". After Aussie and I had got two each and we had taken four into the hospital we realised that it was becoming difficult to keep the fact that at least four of the birds were laying daily. We then divided the days laying between us and the Shoko.

Four weeks later tragedy struck. I went to feed them and found one of them dead. I brought it back to our hut and showed it to the Shoko. He told the guards to dispose of it. The next morning he met me as I came back from feeding them. "Any more chickens bioki" he said. "Yes" I said, "One more bioki (ill), probably die tonight." "Ok you kill bioki one and more one and I have friends to party tonight and we have chicken michi (meal)".

I caught the two and went to find a chopping block on which to behead them. I severed the first ones head quickly and let it go. It ran once round the tip headless before it fell and died. The other one I stuck to until it stopped fluttering. I had visions of my headless chicken falling down a borehole and being lost forever. We plucked and dressed the two birds and cut all the meat from the bones and again kept the bones for boiling up for stew for us and the boys in the hospital.

The chicken bits were fried in coconut oil and mixed with chilli, ready to be put on the stove in the Shoko's hut. The two Jap Officers arrived from a camp nearby and we were given the three bottles to fill with wine from the carboy. As before we managed to sneak a share into our mess tin for consumption later.

The meal was over and we saved any bits that were left to go in our stewpot. Shortly afterwards, the two Japanese girls arrived and were shown into the Officers hut. More wine was asked for and the party seemed to be developing nicely. Suddenly things went wrong. One of the guards from the main gate into the camp came running up and spoke to the Jap Tobang and was sent into the Officers hut. We could see the occupants dashing around tidying up. The girls came out and ran behind the hut led by the guard and were last seen heading for the perimeter fence through the bushes and scrub.

The Japanese told us afterwards that the Secret Police had called at the guardroom and the guard had been despatched to warn the Officers just in case they wanted to search the area. They also confirmed that the Kempi, as the secret police were called, were all powerful and could make demands overriding Officers decisions and enter any camp without permission. Hence the panic situation when they arrived. Apparently they were only enquiring where some other camp was.

One afternoon everyone was away and I expected them all to be away for at least two hours. The forty gallon bath still had hot water in it so I thought I would risk having a grand soak. I could not recall the last time I bathed in hot water. Getting into the drum was quite a feat as the edges where the top had been cut off were quite sharp and there was grave danger you could do yourself a mischief in nasty places. The next move was to sit down in the water so as to be properly submerged. It was quite pleasant being sat in there below the rim level and all one could see was the sky. It also cut off some of the ground insect noises and accentuated the bird calls from the trees.

It would have been better it I'd had any soap and then a rough towel for a rub afterwards, but I had to be content to get dry by standing in the sun for ten minutes. I felt almost civilised for a short time .

The ashes had to be cleared from the hearth underneath the barrel every morning. We of course only burnt timber and if I had put some slightly damp wood on the day before it may still be smouldering the next day. I usually looked if there was any fire left before scraping the ashes out to relay the fire. I looked this particular morning and could not feel or see any lit embers. I stretched my arm out to the back of the hearth and made a scoop out of my hand and withdrew it. A searing pain shot up my arm and I thought I had been burnt and withdrew my hand. I was panic stricken, horrified to see clinging firmly to my right hand index finger, was a small scorpion with its pincers firmly biting my finger.

I shook it off and was going to tread on it and crush the beast but realised I had no shoes on. I held tightly to the arm that had been bitten in the hope of stopping the poison going up the arm. Already I could feel pain under the armpit and I thought of all the stories of the fatality of scorpion bites. I dashed off to the medical hut with all sorts of last wishes, before I died, going through my head. The medical orderly said they had no antidote. He suggested we put my hand in a bowl of hot water. This was provided but I could feel a swelling rising under my arm and the pain was terrific but I was still able to move my arm and fingers. The orderlies thought that a scorpion bite was not always fatal! My arm was put in a sling and I went back to work. The pain eased over the next few hours. Perhaps I am not going to die yet I thought and moved my fingers and arm. The next day I could use my arm with only slight stiffness. Another fatal question answered in the negative.

To be able to go into the water and submerge the whole of ones naked body under the water and rub the dirt from your head was something we had not known since the war started. When we were in Tiaso we could only immerse ourselves up to the waist because of the danger of contracting cholera from the surface water. Soap and towels had long since disappeared and so it was a matter of lounging around until you were dry which would only take some five minutes in the tropical heat. There were always Thai men and women lurking in the jungle on the rivers edge so we had to keep a very close watch on our clothes or they would make a quick dash from the bush and be away with the only clothes you had. Occasionally Thai girls brought fruit to sell but if the Japs saw them talking to us they would be chased away .

On one occasion I bought what I thought was a water melon or similar fruit. I carried it back to the camp looking forward to having a feast of tasty fruit with my cup of rice. I tried to cut it with a knife but I did not even scratch the surface. I dropped it hard on to a stone an d dropped another stone on to it to no avail. I gave up and never did find out what was in it.

When first we moved into our present camp Wakibioshi had somehow obtained an electricity generator. The camp was for the very sick from the other Kanburi camp and he gave instructions that the first place to be lit must be the hut where the most seriously ill men were. For Japanese Officer to make any sacrifice for us as prisoners of war was unheard of and we wondered what could be the reason for the generosity. This was the first time we had seen an electric light since we left Changi almost a year ago.

During the afternoon when we had been down to the river, a piano was delivered and installed in Wakibioshis hut. I was amazed to hear the sound of music coming from the hut and I could just see the top of the piano rocking and swaying on the bamboo floor. I expected it to fall through the floor and perhaps the whole hut to collapse.

In the evening two Japanese girls were escorted by the main gate guards and taken to the "Music Room". Shortly afterwards another Japanese Officer appeared and joined the two who were already at the party. We again had the performance with the wine carboy. Three bottles to fill from the kettle leaving half a pint each for Aussie and I. The party kept calling for more wine and we felt we had drunk enough so the surplus was put into our water bottles. When the wine had been flowing for some time the laughter became more and more maudlin and the piano playing less and less skillful. I had visions of bravely dashing into the falling building and rescuing at least one of the girls and perhaps get a reward!

The party broke up about midnight. We made our way back to our sleeping quarters before the Japs came out. When we got back to our hut we had to creep about in the dark and avoid waking the Japs just over the partition. We shared out a water bottle full of wine with the rest f the hut. I sure slept well that night having enjoyed the fun and the risks of being in trouble.

At this time the guards were leaving Kanburi and being replaced by others fresh up from Singapore. The night before their departure they held a party with lots of music and singing. After their meal which was given to them in buckets they kept the buckets and with a bamboo pole, used them as drums by beating them until they were flat. The guards also brought in a supply of Saki which flowed freely during the evening. It was wise on these evenings to remain within your own hut as a favourite pastime of the Japs was to chase any prisoner who ventured out, and as they were sometimes armed with a bayonet anything could happen. Our Japanese camp Commandant remained with us and so did his Tobang. However, the second Tobang would be replaced by a guard from the new guard. There were usually from a working camp up country and were anxious to get a chance to beat us up just for the hell of it but after a week or so they realised they did not have the backing of the other guard or the Commandant, sullenly gave up their efforts to provoke us.

The railway was now almost complete and many of the men who had survived had gone back down to Singapore and the difficulty in getting food for our camp decided the Japanese to send us back. I was told to help put all the belongings of the Japanese Officers out ready for the move the next day. We were told to fill some bottles from what was left in the big carboy of wine. This we did and the

Jap to whom it belonged counted the bottles and the glass container was to be abandoned .

The next day we were told to report to Wakibioshi to help load the wagon to take it to the station. The man that owned the wine checked the bottles only to find there was one missing. The second Tobang who had only recently joined us and disliked me intensely, told him I had it. The Japanese Officer who had lived in the other part of the kitchen area and was the owner, picked up a bamboo pole which was unfortunately handy. He was looking for me when the Korean Tobang intervened and said that the other Japanese, who was his Tobang had taken it .

Fortunately for me the Korean was believed and the Shoko chased his own Tobang backwards to the other end of the hut all the time hitting him over the head with the bamboo and shouting and swearing at him. He continued the attack when he had nowhere to retreat to. There were marks and weals all over his head and face and another five minutes was spent shouting at him. I was very grateful to the Korean for saving me from a beating probably worse than the Jap guard got .

The piano which we had to load to go back down country proved to be the same one which I last saw when we left it standing at Bam Pong on our up when the band also lost the big drum. I rejoined the rest of the men I had come into the camp with for a march to join the train at Kanchunaburi station. As when we came up we were herded into metal rice trucks with all our gear and camp equipment .

I had been at this camp for about three months and although I had dysentery all the time, I had been able to acquire more food than I would have had, had I not been in the Japanese quarters. This meant that I had gained a little weight and had not been exposed to so much infection .

CHAPTER THIRTEEN

BACK TO SINGAPORE

We entrained at Kanburi station in much the same way as on our journey going up to Thailand. One noticeable difference was the fact that much of the junk which we had when we went up was long since discarded. Many men were on stretchers and had to be lifted from the ground to the height of the wagon floor as we loaded in the goods yard not at the station. The journey down the Malaya peninsula to Singapore gave us hope that things would be better once we arrived at our destination and nothing could be much worse than the past year in Thailand.

When we arrived at Penang, the children were still starving and begging food from us, but all we were given was a small cup of cooked rice. Any damage from the time we were fighting there seemed to have been repaired, but there was an air of desolation about the place. The food we got on the journey was little and seldom and we were continually shunted into sidings whilst Japanese troop trains went by in both directions .

There was a wagon load of Geisha Girls in one of the trucks on our train so we did stop more often than on the up country journey. We were in the usual closed rice wagons. At night we needed to keep the sliding doors open as the stench of rotting flesh and human excrement was stifling. The conditions meant that some of the stretcher cases died and we had to keep the bodies with us till the journeys end in Singapore. I think the journey down took six days but as we did not receive regular meals or drinks, day and night seemed to have no meaning .

Our only thought was to get back to Singapore as soon as possible. On May 1st 1944 we arrived back in Singapore which was for me exactly one year from the day I left.

I had survived. The survivors in this fight for life were not necessarily the big Australian Cattle or Sheep men who were manual workers before the war. The urge to survive seemed to come from the desire to get home to those you loved.

To survive in the circumstances of disease, filth, starvation and ill treatment one needed not just hope for tomorrow but hope for a year or whenever you would get home.

If you had not the will to survive today there was no tomorrow .

The men from this train were sent to various camps in Singapore. I was destined for Kranji. This was a small camp from which the vegetable gardens drew their manpower. It was situated near to the Naval Base at Kepple Harbour.

I was working on the gardens where we grew some vegetable to augment the rations the Japanese allowed us. the main crop was sweet potatoes but instead of letting them grow and produce tubers, our need was so urgent for food to just sustain life that we cut the foliage and used it in a stew. It as least turned the stew green and you could not see the bottom of the bucket. The taste of food was totally ignored. No one ever said "I cannot stand the taste of this, you can have mine". He would have been knocked down in a rush to accept the offer .

We had begun to accept that we never sat on a chair but tended to squat on our haunches when resting. Most men had only one garment, that was a pair of shorts or a G-String. If one got the chance to wash one clothing you stood or squatted within sight of your garment and allowed the fresh air to cleanse your naked body until the clothes were dry .

Now that we were living in proper huts and more attention could be given to the sick and I was beginning to lose more blood from piles than I was producing, I decided to report sick. The M.O. said he would operate on me the next day. Apart from when I had malaria and had been unconscious on and off for a fortnight, I had never fainted or been under anesthetic before and so I was apprehensive about what happened when you passed out. All types of anesthetic were in short supply so the doctors just gave enough to keep you under influence for no longer than they considered the operation required.

I do not remember actually going under and until I started to come round and found myself upside down and hanging straddle legged on what I think was a machine that was used for butchers to hang beasts on while they chopped them into sides of beef down the middle! I heard what appeared to me to be a whisper "He is coming round". Not realising where I was I looked round to see if there were more beasts strung up beside me. Fortunately there were not and as I was quickly swung round and unstrapped and placed back on the operating table. The surgeon told me the operation was not completed but I should leave the continuation until we got home. That same surgeon later received the Military Medal for Bravery, but not for the job he'd done on me! However, as far as I was concerned it was a super job and I am very grateful because once the wound healed the dysentery got better and I felt much better.

We were having American planes flying over on reconnaissance. these continued for three or four days until a lone bomber dropped a few bombs from a great height and one landed near the huts. This terrified the Japanese and we were ordered to dig slit trenches around the guard house and near some of the huts. We had a tropical storm the following morning and everywhere was flooded for a short time. We still had to clear some loose sand out of the bottom of most of the trenches. We deliberately had not made a very good job of the trenches nearest to the guard house. The bombers came over, the siren sounded for an air raid alert about eleven in the morning. The Jap guards came running out of the guard house and jumped, rifles and all in a sort of dive into the nearest dug out. The prisoners mostly waited until the plane came more overhead and of course when it was directly overhead and the bomb doors had not opened we were not in the range of the target .

The all clear sounded and the Japs reappeared with their rifles covered in mud and their uniforms splattered all over and many minus their hats. We made ourselves scarce as they were likely to get rough if we laughed at them and made them lose face.

We were awakened at about five o'clock one morning shortly after the bombers had been over, to the sound of a terrific explosion. The Naval Base was about half a mile away from our camp at Kranji and all sorts of rumours went around as to the cause. Some said the paratroopers had landed, some said that the Navy had shelled the Base. Later in the morning when we went back to work in the gardens, someone found a huge lump of sheared metal and this confirmed something had been blown up. After the war I learned that this was a Limpet Mine, planted by men in miniature submarines, on a destroyer on Keppel Harbour Naval Base.

Events of this kind boosted our morale tremendously and we were prepared to suffer the bombings if it was going to release us sooner. The raids were welcome and were the first sign in three years that we could be within sight of a victory and an end to the war.

After our experiences up country, Kranji was an improvement on any camps we had been in since our capture three and a half years earlier.

During one of my stays in hospital before I moved to Changi Jail, there was a man in the bed opposite me who was ill with dysentery and had also lost his mind. He had lost control of all this functions and was writing about on his bed. In normal circumstances I presume he would have had an injection to calm him down in his last few hours of life. Such comforts were not available and nature had to take its course. Although he was in such an awful state he could speak fairly distinctly. From dawn to the time of his death, about four o'clock in the afternoon he recited the Lords Prayer from beginning to end. Every word was clear and as soon as he finished with "Amen" he started again with "Our Father". The orderlies were helpless and the other patients had to watch the whole dreadful scene as there were not even curtains to screen the bed off.

In another bed was a young man who had been on a work party in Singapore where the rations had been very small. He had developed a disease, common to many, which caused swelling and soreness of the tongue and mouth.

The Japanese had just issued postcards for every prisoner to send home. The message had to be confined to twelve words only.

This young man was having difficulty in writing but had dictated a cheerful message to his mother but we had difficulty in that he could not remember his own address. However, with our help he had completed the card and we handed it in with the rest of the postcards.

Within five minutes the lad fell back on the bed and died. That card would be received by his mother some three months later and she would be so pleased to hear from him. This postcard may have been the first information that her son was alive.

The food situation in Changi was becoming worse. The Japanese provided some fertiliser for us to put on the vegetable gardens. It was awful smelling stuff and on analysis proved to be fish manure. The medics decided it would do us mor e good by being eaten at once rather than wait for the resultant vegetables. The cook house were serving what they called porridge. This was toasted rice boiled and served in a sloppy mess for breakfast. It was decided that the fish manure should be mixed with the porridge so that at least one horrible taste should be substituted by a taste slightly less horrible. It was a desperate effort to keep those of us who were left, alive.

Before the war started in Malaya, the Authorities decided to test a theory, that ordinary powdered lime mixed with dry rice would preserve it from being consumed by rats and weevils. This had remained in stock all through the war and the Japanese would not eat it. They decided to issue it to us in place of the ordinary ration of rice. We had no option but to accept and use it. Again all through it was so awful to the taste that we had difficulty in swallowing it, it was a matter of eating it or dying of starvation. We ate it.

An entry in my "Log Book" for March 11th 1945: New low rice ration of seven ounces per day per man. Three ounces of vegetables and half an ounce of dried fish. These were the weights before the rations had been washed, or the fish cleaned.

Breakfast consisted of about three quarters of a pint of cooked rice made as a sort of porridge and served with a three quarter size pint mug and to ensure we all got an equal amount the server had a knife and sliced off any "top". At midday we had a cup of tea and a small rice bun. In the evening there was fish soup and two rissoles made of rice and fried. There was no milk, sugar or salt. I understand the total consumption of food per person in England was about 2 lbs

9 ounces per day.

The longing for a good meal never left us and was the greatest item in our conversation. This occasionally awoke anger and frustration and someone would threaten to punch the next man that talked about food. This we knew was no idle threat and food would not be mentioned again until the next meal time.

The camp at Kranji was closed and we then moved to Changi Jail. I was first housed in what I should imagine was normally the dining room. The cells were all occupied by three or more men and others were sleeping on the wire mesh stretched across at each floor level. The Jail was intended for 600 prisoners, but the Japanese put 6,000 men in and every available space was utilised and we were thick on the ground .

I was again put into hospital with dysentery. We still had very little medicine and the only help was a less rough diet. At one time we were served as an experiment stewed grass. This was awful and made me much worse. I developed scabies and these became septic and it was not until I was unable to hold a spoon as my fingers were locked that I got any treatment. The medical man I was under was in charge of the dysentery ward and scabies came under skin diseases. I was not fit to transfer but it was only after pleading that I could no longer feed myself that the skin doctor was asked to see me. Incidentally the skin ward was only a floor below.

I was stretchered to an area which had been bombed. The building itself was completely demolished but there where two ordinary baths complete with running water and the orderlies had a brazier with a large cauldron on and heated the water to nearly boiling. We then stripped and were scrubbed with stiff brushes until most of the worse sores were bleeding. We then had to soak in the bath with hot water and disinfectant for about half an hour.

It so happened that where we were almost on top of a hill at the side of the jail and as we were being scrubbed we could see almost the whole of Singapore. The site was actually a demolished bath house with nothing left but the concrete base with two ordinary domestic baths in it. In spite of the terrible pain of the scrubbing and the soaking in the hot bath, the magnificent view of the main harbour and out to the sea, was worth all the hassle. With the temperature around

100 degrees in the sun I would have liked to stay there until sundown.

I often wondered what people thought to see these two baths way out in the open country and see men getting out of them and as we had no towels we just stood around naked until we dried off.

The treatment certainly worked and within a few days I was pronounced fit to leave the hospital area and go back to the jail. I now weighed only seven stone. I was put on to the gang who were splitting huge logs with axes and wedges hammered in with a fourteen pound hammer. Although this was hard physical labour I put on weight through the development of muscle. I had only short trousers and the sun burnt my feet and legs as I had no shoes, and my feet were not hardened after being in hospital. The sun had caught the tender skin on my legs swollen with Beri-Beri. Again I was back in hospital with Solar Dermititus and Beri-Beri.

After about a week in hospital out of the sun I was again discharged and went back to the woodyard. The timber we cut up was for burning on the fires in the cookhouse. The cooking went on almost continuously and they used many tons of logs. After about a fortnight working in the timber yard I gained strength and as we were not bothered by the Japanese guards, we were not rushed.

The Japanese were very short of petrol and we were never allowed a motorised vehicle to bring in the logs from the forest. Instead they provided us with a captured Marman Truck which was normally a very heavy four wheel drive vehicle which could be used on heavy terrain. The instructions from them was "pull it yourself".

It was then stripped down, the engine removed, cab removed, gearbox taken out and everything that we could manage without was removed to lighten the weight. The "power unit" was a rope attached to the front towing hook with bamboo bars fastened to the rope at about yard and a half intervals with provision for five men power or more at each side of the rope and a leader at the front. With this timber wagon, we set off for the woodland about three miles from the jail. We had a Japanese guard with us who rode shotgun sitting crosslegged and with his rifle across his knees, on the lorry platform.

This was my first experience on this outing. the lead man at the front would give the signal to go and everyone had to pull with an even pull or you could pull your even number backwards if you started too soon. We managed to get on to the main road with a lot of cursing each other for not keeping in unison. Once on the smooth surface of the road, we trotted steadily on what was a flat stretch and then as we came to a hill we had to put our full weight into every stride and at last reached the top of the rise. The Jap said "All men rest". We lay down at the side of the road absolutely exhausted and dreading the order to move again. Five minutes and came the order "Speedo all man. Curra". We had made sure before stopping that we had actually got over the rise so that everyone could climb aboard before we set off down the hill.

There was very little traffic except for a few bicycles and the odd Japanese truck, as petrol for the civilian population was in ultra short supply. "All aboard" was the shout to the driver to release the brake. The faster we went down the hill the further the impetus would take us up the hill we were heading for. So to the song of "She'll be coming down the mountain" we went faster and faster to the bottom of the hill and we had to judge the time to jump off and take up the rope before the wagon lost too much speed ascending the next hill.

It was a scramble to get into your correct position and take up the slack on the rope as fast as possible and pull as hard as you could as there could be no stop until we reached the brow of the hill. With the shouts and curses of the guard and knowing that any slacking would mean a crack across the bare back with a bamboo pole every man summed up unbelievable strength. This went on over the three miles or so to the woodlands.

When we got onto the forest road, as it was monsoon season, there were great pools and deep ruts in the roads. We came to some tree roots which were some four feet across and four feet high. These we had to dig out and chop the roots off until they could be heaved out of the soil. As far as I could figure there was no way we could lift these onto the truck. However the guard thought differently. We put two tree trunks as planks from the ground to the lorry and slide them onto the wagon. It was unbelievable what power can be extracted out of a dozen human wrecks when threatened by a bamboo pole and a rifle butt. We had a large platform on this wagon and the Jap forced us to load three huge roots and part trunks onto our wagon. The timber would weigh at least six tons. We had great difficulty in getting the truck under way when we finished loading as it had sunk into the ground with the sheer weight of the load.

In spite of it being obvious that we were going to have trouble getting started the guard climbed aboard and sat on the front tree trunk to ride "shotgun". We pushed, we shoved, we heaved and pulled but the truck moved not an inch. We tried levering under the tyres but to no avail. The suggestion was made that the driver turn the front wheels full lock and with alot of help from the tree trunks used as levers the wheels were turned full lock away from the roadside. We then all pulled on the rope at an angle of the wheels to try and move the front wheels out of the rut.

Very slowly there was some movement and we gave a big cheer. However the load started to shift and we could see the back near side wheel slowly leaving the ground. With a great noise of the ropes snapping the whole wagon turned on its side, the three great tree trunks toppled over into a ditch. We had to stifle our great joy at seeing the Imperial Japanese Guard flung headlong into the bushes, rifle and all. It seemed worthwhile at first but then we realised we would have to rebuild the whole lot .

Our experience of loading the first time stood us in great stead and we reloaded much quicker. We had put the truck on a solid piece of ground and with a tremendous effort we were underway again.

The return journey was even more hazardous. We had a load of some six tons plus the weight of the truck to pull. We were so anxious to get as far as possible up the hills the driver was reluctant to brake and we took some corners almost on two wheels. It was also more difficult to jump aboard for the downhill runs with having great lumps of tree root hanging over the side of the truck. Fortunately there was little traffic on the roads.

Any cyclist we saw went on to the grass verge and fled into the rubber plantation. The bullocks in the carts stampeded as we sped at high speed silently by and caused a sudden wind pressure. It was the most thrilling ride I have ever had. By the time we got back to the jail I was exhausted. I was barefooted and the mud had got between my toes in the bush and had hardened as we had got onto the tarred road. By midday the roads were beginning to melt and the tar stuck to my feet. We had been out since eight o'clock and it was midday before we got back. The midday meal consisted of one cup of tea and fried rice rissole but no sugar or milk in the tea.

We were out again in the afternoon for another load. Apart from the night marches to Thailand I had never felt so utterly tired and miserable. I was on this party for about ten days and we went out every other day, twice a day. It was then taken over by another party.

Occasionally I was on a party that went for the rations for the Japanese cookhouse. This meant going with a much smaller truck which had been stripped down to be pulled by manpower. We went with two Japanese guards to Changi village to buy sweet potatoes, yams, eggs, chickens etc. We went on this trip with shirts on so that if we got the chance, we could pick up the odd potato and slip it inside the shirt, but you always risked being beaten up if you were caught.

CHAPTER FOURTEEN

THE STAND BY PARTY

I was put on a party called Stand By Party. Our duty was to be ready to take on any task that was out of the run of everyday work in the night or during the day. At the time I was sleeping in the jail and went to the standby hut after breakfast and joined the rest of the gang and waited for some call from perhaps the Japs. It may be to unload a truck bringing rice in which case we put shirts on and hoped to get a few grains of rice into our pockets if they fell on the ground .

Whilst Living in the jail, I noticed that a sparrow was building a nest at the top of a girder in the passage. I realised I had no hope of catching the sparrow and eating it, they never got much to eat themselves they were so thin, but I thought it would lay two or three eggs and I could wait until it had laid. I watched the nest building as the birds went to and fro with nesting material, and then I decided the time was ripe to strike. I climbed up some wire mesh and just managed to get my fingers into the nest and withdrew two eggs. When I was in Kanburi the Japanese had candles and if there was a breeze the tallow ran down on to a table or wherever they had the candle. I gathered it up and served it .

Later I found a small tin and melted all the tallow and put a strand of old rope in the centre for a wick and had a very valuable asset. I broke the eggs into my mess tin and found both of them were half way to hatching. I stalled at the thought of eating them raw in that state but I could not bring myself to throw such tasty morsels of food away. My survival instinct said there was nourishment there. Again

I had saved matches which I had acquired from the Japs. The day before I had managed to conceal a very small sweet potato from the Jap rations. I had no water to wash it with but I cut in into small pieces and melted some tallow into the bottom of the mess tin. I then held the tin over the night light and after about twenty minutes the tallow began to fry a little bit but after half an hour one could hardly call the potatoes chips. I ate the egg, chicken and chips and considered it the most horrible meal I'd had for some time but it was food and even minute quantities of food were welcome to augment our starvation diet .

There was a small courtyard within the jail and anyone who had managed to get under the showers when the water was turned on usually washed anything they had to wear. There had been some washing stolen from the line so the Sergeant detailed everyone to take a turn as "Guard of the Washing". The day I was on one man complained that he hung a pair of underpants and when he came to me for them they were missing.

I maintained I had not seen them on the line. However he insisted and my bed space was searched to no avail. I was put on a charge and the next day duly appeared before the Commanding Officer. The charge was negligence on duty whilst in charge of Army kit. I was given a hat so that it could be taken from me as I stepped up to answer the "grave" charge.

My answer was "Inview of the fact that very few men had any underpants and I would be conspicuous if I wore the only pair in the jail I was not likely to take them if they were ever on the line." This was typical of the hilarious things that authority was prepared to do and I found it difficult to restrain my amusement of the whole charade. The charge was dismissed but my friends had a good laugh about it.

There were rumours about that the Japs were building an airfield in Singapore and it was not very long before the first party was named to work there. The site chosen was a swamp and a lot of the filling had already been done. The Prisoners of War were brought in to move sand from the perimeter to the runways and level it all off.

I was on the gang scheduled to go the next week. I always felt glad that no move could be much worse and therefore in an odd sort of way looked forward to the change.

We had to parade at 7.00 a.m. and were issued with a fill of our water bottles. The site was two or three miles from the jail and of course we had to walk. When we arrived we were issued with a shovel each and sent to the perimeter of the airfield. We had to dig sand from the dunes and fill up the trucks, which then took the load to dump it for a large gang of Tamils, Malays, Chinese and Japanese to fill their baskets and put them on their heads to carry to the edge of the part which was to be levelled.

After filling a few loads we realised that the Japanese guard had moved away from us and sat down in the shade and when he could see the sand piled up over the side he shouted "O.K." and waved the driver to move off. We had been loading from both sides of the wagon and somebody realised we could load from the side in view of the guard and have half the gang resting at the other side. This meant that we could send the truck off with only half a load. We were working with two trucks and this meant we were not keeping the other truck waiting. The truck drivers were Australians and they promised to take the load a long way round and if the Japs said anything they were to say they would sink and get stuck in certain parts and they were driving to avoid the areas where they might get stuck.

Until the break at noon we were in full glare of the sun and could not find shelter. We were allowed, at lunch time, to get some shade under the palm trees, but there were so many men trying to get some shade that it was not easy to find a shady place. We were allowed to make some tea, and we were issued with a small rice cake from the jail cookhouse and that had to last until 6.00 p.m. when we arrived back at the jail.

We had some Aussies to work with us one day and it took ages to convince them that we were delaying the job as much as possible because the sooner it was finished, the sooner it would be used by the Jap Airforce for their fighter aircraft. This fact was visibly brought to our attention when two of the Jap planes came down and tried to run us down as we were working. All in its path had to run to escape being killed by the wheels as they actually touched the ground and flew off again.

We had to work carrying the sand in baskets the same as the Tamils, Indian women, Chinese collies and Chinese girls. We noticed that they too were up to all sorts of time wasting tactics.

Sometimes on our way back to camp we had a tropical storm and it was great fun to feel the cool rain on our tired and sun scorched bodies .

We were often not able to get a shower until ten or eleven at night as the water pressure to the jail was not strong enough to reach us during the day .

After a few weeks the main runway was finished and the Japs had us levelling mounds of sand which had been piled up at night by the only mechanical digger they had. We questioned a guard about this and he told us his Officers wanted to prolong the job as long as they could because they were expecting to be sent to the Burma Front as soon as the aerodrome was finished. It was a small wonder they were not rushing us .

The Japanese reduced the number of men called for the aerodrome job and I went back to work with the Standby Party. We used a small hut which was outside the jail itself but rather isolated and had a narrow path running at one side. There was a post at the far side of the path and a wire stretched rather loosely to one of the bamboo poles which were the main supports for the corners of the bamboo framework .

We were all in the hut waiting for a call one morning when the Japanese guard went by with the bayonet fixed on his rifle and carrying it on his shoulder. The bayonet struck the wire and I noticed a Sergeant who was not actually on the Standby Party but was in our hut to speak to our Sergeant was anxious not to be seen in our hut. The guard uttered a few swear words and went on his way. At this point we were told to always, at the approach of the guard, pick up the brush from the corner of the hut and appear to be sweeping up if the Jap came into the hut room.

We used this wire to hang out any washing we had been able to do and at the time there was a pair of shorts fastened to it. Years later at a reunion I learnt that the wire was an aerial and the brush had a wireless receiver in the head. If the Japanese had discovered the truth at least some of us would have been executed and the rest of us beaten up and put into solitary confinement. The fact that you did not know would not have been accepted as a defence by the Japanese Officers.

The contents of the broadcasts that our men heard were not given out to the general body of troops but kept for a day or two and only released when there had been time to have been told through other sources than the radio. Having a radio was one of the worst crimes we could commit and was usually punished with death. Those who were responsible for the building and operation of them were brave men indeed. When we surrendered, anyone with access to radio parts was told to take anything that could help build a receiver and would be unlikely to attract the attention of the guards, into captivity with them. All these parts gradually came together in the prison and other parts made from pieces of metal formed the main source of information coming into the camps.

I was in the hut we used as a base for the Standby Party, probably about the last week in August, when a Japanese Orderly from the Commanding Officers Headquarters in Changi Jail demanded; "One soldier to Shoko Office very quick". The command was given as if he had something to fear if there was no-one available. I was the only man there, apart from the Sergeant, left on duty. "Right Wilson see what he wants" said the Sergeant. The Japanese guard turned to me and in the usual abrupt manner said, "Ok. You come quick Speedo. Speedo". I was rushed up the stairs to the Head Office on the top floor following closely in the Nips footsteps. I was apprehensive as to what was going to happen as sometimes they would just pick on anyone to beat up .

I was ushered into the Office and amidst much bowing by all concerned I was stood to attention in front of the Commandants desk. This is really serious I thought, as it was not usual for any prisoner of war to be allowed in the Office. I had fleeting visions of being be-headed as an example to all others to behave or, at least to go back to the Unit with some exterior damage to my person. There was a pause whilst the Shoko signed some documents and I was really getting worked up about getting "worked over". "You know Japanese Flag on pole over prison?" He said. "Yes" I replied relieved by the reasonable tone of his voice. "You go on roof of jail and take Flag off pole and bring into my Office." He then resumed his paper work. The Jap guard accompanied me to the stairs leading to the flat roof but made no effort to follow. The Flag was on the tower at the front gates.

I have always had an aversion to heights and tend to lose my balance when even on the edge of a cliff or up a ladder. This job, I thought could be a disaster for me. The main roof was surrounded by a low wall but there was a kind of turret up in the centre. The flag was flying gently in the breeze. Before climbing the iron runged ladder to the base of the pole, I made sure that the guard was not watching as it was a long drop to the ground!

The view from this very high vantage point was breathtaking. I could see out to sea over the harbour and on either side the islands near Singapore. Almost the whole of Singapore town was visible.

I could have enjoyed the view for a long time, but the longer I put off climbing the last few rungs of the ladder the more jittery I would become. I braced myself to get on a small platform at the base of the flag pole to undo the cord to wind the flag down. With a few snags, as the wind took it in the wrong direction, I was able to make the cords fast and remove the flag. I screwed it up irreverently and tucked the bulk under my arm. I decided it would be safer folding it when I was on the main part of the roof.

I began to think. Here I am lowering the Japanese flag, what a joy it would be if it was an omen and was for real and for always. I spread it out on the roof and there in the centre was the dreaded symbol of the rising sun which had meant nearly four years of torment and cruelty and starvation and death to so many of my friends. If only I could have lowered it for the last time.

I took a step and put one foot on the sun and twisted my foot to grind into that omen everything I hated about it. I brought the other foot forward and jumped up and down in anger at all that poached egg meant to me. Even as now I relive the incident it affects me profoundly. I had another look at the view, calmed down and carefully folded the large flag and descended from the tower.

The Nip guard was waiting for me at the bottom of the steps. He then accompanied me back to the Nippon Office. I was told to deposit the flag in a corner of the Office and was made to understand that it was going away for cleaning. I looked often in the next fourteen day to see if the flag was flying again. It was never put up again and I was at the little ceremony after the Japanese surrender of hoisting the Union Jack on that same pole and mentally recalled my private incident on the roof of the prison and that I had lowered the Japanese flag for the last time after all .

The guard escorted me all the way back to our hut and made no attempt to speak and I was glad of this as the mood I was in may have shown itself in any attempt at conversation.

The atmosphere in the jail and the general attitude of the prisoners was now much calmer and after three and a half years grumbling about food and conditions, we became, I thought, less and less miserable.

Those who were still surviving began to have some hop of getting out alive. Previously the most optimistic thought we had perhaps a fifty fifty chance of getting home. In the evenings we used to gather in the inner area of the prison with friends and talk sometimes until well after midnight. The Japanese guards never came into the jail after dark, I think they felt they may never go out again if they did.

We had long arguments about politics, religion, wives, children, sport, our jobs and our prospects when we arrived back home. In spite of the suffering most of these men were hardened by their experiences.

We began to learn to learn of successes of our troops in Europe, of the death of Mussolini, and that some of the Pacific Islands had been retaken and that the Burma Front was improving.

A number of us went out most days to dig holes in the hillside near to the jail. We made an entrance of about five foot high and three or four yards into the hillside and then hollowed out a chamber as large as we could without the roof caving in on us.

Some of the guards gave us to understand that many of these were to be dug and if the British invaded Singapore or Malays all prisoners of war from the jail would be forced into these holes and the entrance would be blown up with hand grenades. This threat was confirmed by a number of guards and also civilians who were also working on this site .

We were not allowed to talk to civilians. However one day when we were having a break there was a young Malay trying to attract my attention without being seen by the guard. We were both on a ledge near the entrance to the funk holes. He squatted down with his back to me and I moved out of site of our guard and squatted down as close as I dare with my back to him. He half turned his head and whispered. "Soon very good news. Maybe war over soon. You keep quiet." As the day went on I had been telling all the gang what I had been hearing from the Malayan man. The Japanese guards appeared apprehensive and were allowing us much longer breaks and the frantic rush they had for us to dig our graves seemed to have diminished .

When we arrived back at the jail and heard that they too had heard that good news was on the way, we really felt there may be some truth but so many rumours had circulated in the past that we were always sceptical. However, in the evening before roll call we were told to carry on everything as normal and work would go on the following day as usual. The next day we had heard of this powerful new atomic bomb that had been dropped on Hiroshima.

The Japs cancelled all work parties and still we were told to keep calm and not provoke any trouble with the guards. A number of us stayed late into the night talking in the jail yard. I could not sleep and eventually got up and went down the corridor to the lavatory. The cookhouse staff worked all through the night as the kitchens were not large enough to cater for so many men at one cooking. One of the cooks came in to the loo and told me that Japan had asked for peace terms and a cease-fire had been agreed.

In view of the rumour I had heard at work the day before and knowing that radio contact with Rangoon was more likely to be established during the night I felt optimistic.

I returned to my bedspace in the main hall of the jail in a daze of hope and also fear that it may not be true. Everyone was sound asleep and all was quiet. The full moon cast its brilliant beams across the floor and accentuated the bars high up the walls. Total piece seemed to reign over the area. I sat down on the blanket which was the only bedding I had and with head in hands all sorts of possibilities passed through my mind .

If I awakened any of my friends this could result in a reaction to the news of wild excitement and could end in a noisy chatter and even some cheering and sufficient noise to disturb the guards outside the jail gates. Their reaction might cause a riot and panic firing on us and a loss of life at a time when we were nearer to freedom than we had been over three and a half years. I lay down and promptly went to asleep. I awoke at the usual time in the morning and apparently no-one had heard the news. Within a few minutes our Sergeant came in and called us together and told us that there could be some very good news but we were to parade as usual for work parties and act as is we knew nothing .

The Japanese guards were ill at ease and the usual roll call was taken but it was obvious that they were very worried. The guards kept well away from us and we gave them no provocation. No-one was risking their life by causing trouble and we were happy that we had something to look forward to and did not expect instant freedom.

There was an area in the centre of the jail building itself which was normally, I presume, the exercise yard. Here, after lights out at ten o'clock, we were in the habit of gathering for a quiet chat when we knew no Japanese could overhear us. The only thing to disturb us were the mosquitoes. It was particularly pleasant on a moonlit evening.

We really did have something to talk about this night and we stayed chatting until well after midnight. After our ordeal of the past years, the atmosphere was cheerful but not exuberant. We were prepared to wait until we had more certain confirmation of our freedom and the cessation of hostilities .

One of the few possessions I still had, which I managed to retain, was an old army exercise book in which I had written down alot of thoughts which went through my mind. It was really a substitute for not being able to write letters to my wife. I made the following entry when I first realised there was good news about.

"August 11th 1945. We have been told to carry on as usual but there is a very strong rumour of very good news. I do hope it is true. Every week, Every day, every hour seems longer and longer. I hope to be home quickly but many people talk of months of recuperation and acclimatisation before we reach England. Give me a seat in a plane to Ringway tomorrow and I am right in it."

The next entry reads as follows; written in large letters:

"August the Twelfth Nineteen Hundred and Forty Five: Sunday.
We are officially free again. I am too excited to realise it. Three and a half years of waiting, hungry, thirsty, starved and ill and lack of liberty and now freedom and hopes of home soon." I also wrote "I am a

lucky man. I have no bitterness against anyone now. I am at peace with the world, my enemies, those who I dislike. I am prepared to forget the past. All men are my friends. What had been is past. A new life opens out, of love, charity, forgiveness and deep understanding. Farewell to prisons, barbed wire, sentries, compulsory working parties, hunger pangs. I am Duncan Hubert Wilson again and not Signalman number 2595753. I feel I have become a human again. It is like shaking off a disease. "

All this was written in the euphoria of my new freedom. I was later to change some of these sentiments, as life goes on it does not always improve, and thoughts of a new world where everything would now be better, fade away.

During the next two or three days some Allied planes flew over Singapore and the Japanese Anti Aircraft guns opened up and we could see the shells bursting around our aircraft. We were a little worried about this as it was confirmation of a rumour that the Japanese Command in Singapore was threatening to ignore the Cease Fire agreed with Tokyo. However, when the firing was over and the planes had departed, we were still remarkably optimistic and not unduly worried.

By August 18th 1945 we were still under the jurisdiction of the Japanese guards. There were no British troops to take over the general policing of Singapore and until some arrived, we were in no fit state to take control. By now we were beginning to be very impatient and nobody seemed to be doing anything about it.

As a member of the Standby Party I was working outside the jail as escort for those prisoners the Japanese were bringing in from various small camps around Singapore island. Most of these men arrived at the jail on foot and had marched from the other camps. I was the first to greet one man who was pulling a four wheel truck with all his possessions stacked neatly on it. He was totally unaware of the peace moves and his first question was "Whats the grub like here." I told him we were free and I was to show him his Billet. He did not believe me until someone else came up and told him it was true. Once he was convinced he threw his hat into the air and danced round his little truck load of all he possessed. Many who came from outside these camps had been told nothing of the cease-fire and thought they were just being moved once more. It was good to be able to tell them we were free again .

The next day the Allied planes came over and were fired on by the Japanese. It may have been that some Japanese units had not been advised of the cease-fire. Their communication system was very primitive and sometimes consisted of the guard on one camp shouting an air raid warning to the next camp.

About six of us were called out the next day. The Japanese gave us a truck and told us to take it to the aerodrome we had been building and wait for some Allied planes coming over and dropping supplies for us to pick up. We parked the truck in the middle of a small concrete runway and spread ourselves around as conspicuously as possible.

The sky was clear of clouds and we could see for miles. We were beginning to get a little despondent when two tiny specs appeared high in the sky. We were worried incase they were fired on and went away again. They passed over at a fairly high level and we danced and jumped and waved as they passed. All was quiet. We just stared at the receding hope of something to eat. Both planes turned and gradually lined up to come lower over us. Cheers went up and we felt saved again. As they neared us we could see the men in the body of the plane with side doors open and as they neared, the dropping ground containers were pushed out and plummeted towards us.

The first one burst open when it hit the concrete runway. We ran to it as butter splashed around on the concrete. We scooped the butter up with bare hands and greedily stuffed it into our mouths and spat out bits of sand and concrete. It was delicious. To me this was one of the best days I had enjoyed since we were taken prisoners nearly four years before.

As the planes came over on a final run the crew were stood at the doors. Suddenly a figure was pushed out and dropped quickly towards us. It was apparently a man in Air Force uniform and his parachute was not going to open. We all ran to where he was going to land and expected a horrible sight when we got there. The Crew had stuffed a uniform with rags and grass and tied a hat to it. We had been fooled right until we actually reached it.

The cheering which met us when the men back at the jail realised what was in the containers was deafening. We had some of the food through the cookhouse that night. We had almost forgotten what it was like to eat something which tasted nice.

Again on the morning of 31st August the Japanese called on the Standby Party to go to the airfield and await a further drop from the air. The same six men that had been on the trip before were detailed together with a Sergeant. we were provided with a truck with an engine in it and some petrol. We set off in high glee and with the blessing of every man in the jail camp. We on the party were singing and laughing all the way to the airfield.

We parked in the middle of the landing strip and spread ourselves around so that we would hope to be seen clearly from the air. We waited and after half an hour or more, we began to feel apprehensive that something may have gone wrong. What a terrible thing if the Japanese had decided to open fire as they had done earlier in the week when a Reconnaissance Plane from the R.A.F. came over. We consoled ourselves with the thought that they had allowed the drop the day before.

It was now midday and the sun was at its hottest and we had nothing to drink. We were expecting them to come from the same direction as the previous planes and first one and then another shouted "Here they come!" as two dots appeared in the sky heading directly towards us. We jumped on the truck and left them a clear area to drop in and then made our way back on foot to the concrete runway. They did a low run in and circled to make sure of a friendly welcome before gaining height so that the parachutes would have time to open as they dropped. On the first run over, large torpedo like steel objects were jettisoned and landed with a crash on the ground. Some burst open and we rushed to gather the spilled contents of butter, cheese, tinned jam and cigarettes. Whatever butter was on the tarmac we scooped up with our hands and ate it. It was a bit gritty but was Manna from heaven to us. They took another circle and gained more height.

As the first plane came over the far end of the runway we saw a figure leaving the plane and free fall and then the parachute opened and sure enough it was a live man. He was followed by another man and as the plane past over four more men were dropped.

I rushed along with another of the welcoming party to see the first liberator down. Although he fell heavily he said he was fine but badly shaken as he had never done a parachute drop before! The first thing he did was undo his water bottle and take a deep swig. He then offered me a drink and I too took a deep swig and nearly collapsed. It was neat brandy and I coughed and spluttered with tears rolling down my cheeks as we had hardly tasted alcohol for over three years.

I soon recovered and as we waited for the truck to pick up the containers and us, he told me his story. He was a Medical Officer and had been brought out of the Mess in Rangoon, the night before and told "You will be dropped from the air on to a new airfield at Changi Singapore in the morning. Take as many medical things with you as you can muster and also take a Medical Orderly with you." This was at the Air Force base at Rangoon. He said he remonstrated that he had never done a parachute jump before but the R.A.F. assured him he had nothing to fear. That assurance he said had very little effect on his being frightened all the way from Rangoon.

The other four men dropped were, a man from the Returned Allied Prisoners of War Echelon who sole duty was to further the return of all P.O.W.'s to their homes, two Medical Orderlies and another doctor, and the last was a War Correspondent who was a top reporter for the B.B.C. Radio named Willis. One of these dropped on the roof on a bungalow at the edge of the 'drome, but appeared to be none the worse for his fall.

The journey back to Changi on the truck was enlivened by questions from both sides. There were far more questions than answers and as we neared the jail the truck was mobbed by our own men wanting news of home and offering a tremendous welcome to men from the outside world. I never saw these men again but I am still grateful for their courage in coming in, not knowing what their reception by the Japs would be. I count that pick up as one of the most satisfying jobs I had done in the past three and a half years.

September 1st 1945. All those men who were fit enough assembled in the courtyard of the jail and a radio and loud speaker installed. For the first time in three and a half years I heard the radio direct from London. We had the News followed by Sandy MacPherson gave us a talk on a new education programme for the Army, but the greatest reception was given for Francis Day singing "A Nightingale Sang in Berkley Square". The atmosphere was tremendous to think that we had all been prisoners for nearly four years and now we would shortly be leaving for home.

There was also a special broadcast for Far East Prisoners of War. I wrote in my log book (still with the same indelible pencil I had carried all throughout Malaya, Thailand and back to Singapore but was now only one and a half inches long) "Days go by, it is now three weeks yesterday since we heard of Japans surrender and I am still in the same place. Only the atmosphere of freedom is different. We hope to see Mountbattens Fleet here on September 5th and then perhaps we shall fly home to you".

September 3rd.Entry in Log. "Have had quite an exciting day again. More supplies were dropped on Changi aerodrome and I went on the party to pick them up. Its great watching the planes disgorging the load from underneath the rear of the plane. They drop gently and little stuff is damaged. Later in the day five more men were dropped while we were actually on the 'drome. One man fell in a ditch and slightly sprained his ankle but we soon had his gear off and we was able to walk to the pick up truck. The name I have in my log is Major Steele. He also allowed us a swig from his water bottle but this time I think it was rum. He also gave us a Woodbine cigarette each which caused a lot of dizziness and coughing. I am now hoping to get home to you all very quickly. The food is better here now with the Red Cross stuff. "

The Red Cross stuff I was writing about was tinned food that the Japanese had refused to give us which had been in stock in Singapore from the first time and the only Red Cross ship that came to Singapore in the early part of our capture. Had this been distributed at that time it would have saved hundreds of lives. The Japs felt very guilty about this and insisted we bury all the tins when empty and use them up before the British troops arrived! They must have thought we would not mention the fact that they had held on to this food when men were dying daily of starvation.

September 4th 1945. Rumours abounded that the Royal Navy had arrived in Singapore. The following day about twenty of us went down into Singapore to help unload some food from the Naval Support ships. We went aboard one ship and found various tins of fruit, jam, and corned beef lying around and put them into our jackets to take back to the men. However there were Sikh troops on guard and they took them off us before we left the ship. This was particularly galling as the Sikhs in the prison camp went over to the Japanese as soon as we were capitulated and were not very popular with us.

The Navy decided we really were too weak to help them and told us to go and have a look round Singapore. This we did. We were desperate for a drink but we knew the water was suspect. Three of us came across half a dozen men from a Yorkshire Regiment who had just come in that day with the Invasion Force. "Where can we get a cup of tea" we asked. "Well we have tea" they replied, "but we have no way of getting boiling water". "There is plenty of timber around why not make a fire and brew up" we suggested. "We have nothing to put the water in on the fire" was the reply. We seemed to be getting nowhere and no tea. We went to their truck and took a can of petrol and poured it away down the gutter. We then found a water main that was burst but still flowing. Filled the empty can and rinsed it out. We borrowed a hammer and some cutters and took the top off the can and filled it up with water. We soon had a fire place built with all the masonry that was lying about. It was not long before the water was boiling and we all had slightly petrol flavoured tea. The hammer soon opened a tin of condensed milk that the Army found. It was not long before we were surrounded by little children begging for anything that was spare. The incident showed how our experience had taught us to never think that obstacles are insurmountable if the necessity is there.

I had written in my journal on April 4th 1945. !I expect to be home between September 1st and October 1st this year." The time was dragging and frustrating and we had been "free" for nearly three weeks and were still living in Changi jail.

I was delighted to be called out again to receive more food and medical supplies which we were in desperate need of. One metal container was filled with packets of cigarettes, cigarette papers and odd tins of food and even some loose sweets thrown in. Some of the packets had been open and part of the contents were gone. We thought to loot supplies on the way to us who had been without so many things for so long was mean. Two or three years later I met an ex-R.A.F. man who had been stationed at the Base where these supplies had been sent from and he asked me if we got some part used packets of cigarettes and things from one of the containers. "Well" he said, "we heard about this drop when we were in the mess the night before and everybody emptied their pockets into a sack and they dropped it in an extra container! "

The following day we had a very welcome visit from Lord Mountbatten who arrived at the jail in a jeep. I happened to be near the Lieutenant who was incharge of us when we came out of England. As Lord Mountbatten passed us, one of the tyres blew with a tremendous bang. The escorting car stopped and he got into it for the remainder of his journey to the jail gates which was about two hundred yards away. A Senior Officer saw the Signals Officer and ordered him to have the tyre changed. He ordered me to help with the repair and we drew to the side of the road and jacked up the vehicle and changed the wheel as quickly as we could .

In the search for tools and the jack we found a tin of cheese which had been opened but seemed fresh enough. The Officer met my hungry look and said "I don't think this will be missed" and broke the remaining piece in half and we each stuck our share into our pockets. "Better make sure the wagon's alright and give it a test run. Jump in." He said. We did two laps of the outer road of the jail to the cheers of the crowd and then caught up with the VIP's at the outer jail gates. Life was fun again and I was pleased to be a survivor.

We were pleased to hear that an important person was to visit us the next day. This proved to be Lady Mountbatten. We appreciated this visit as we had not seen a British woman for over three years and she was taking some risk as there may have been some Japanese units in Singapore who had not known of the cease fire or were prepared to ignore it .

The Army and the Navy went ahead with the invasion of Singapore and the mainland of Malaya and many lives were lost when troops were wading ashore. There were still men dying of malnutrition and ulcers every day. These deaths seemed so much more sad when freedom was so close by .

Since we had come down from Thailand, a burial had always been followed by Buglers sounding the Last Post. Whenever I hear it for a Military Funeral I think of the times I heard it in Changi. It was now over three weeks since the cease-fire and the surrender ceremony was signed. Time was dragging and we were anxious to be on our way home .

On September 10th 1945, we were officially told we would be boarding a ship for a direct journey home to Liverpool. Sailing also that day would be another ship going to Southampton and there was to be some rivalry between the two Captains as to who would get the first batch of ex-prisoners home to Britain.

We were told to be ready to leave for the docks at five the next morning. We had been issued with fresh khaki drill uniforms. Some of the shorts were Japanese but to have fresh clean clothes was a further step towards civilisation.

We left the jail about ten o'clock on the morning of the 11th September 1945. As we passed through Singapore we were pleased to see Chinese Police and Indian troops in charge of Japanese Prisoners of War who were sweeping the streets.

We boarded the troopship Monawa and were soon under way. As we sailed up the Malacca Straits we could see troop ships still landing on the coast of Malaya.

The food on the ship was specially prepared for us. To have gone on to a full diet most of us realised we could kill ourselves by greediness. In fact before we left Singapore one man had foolishly consumed a tin of condensed milk and it had killed him. Along with a light diet I ate two pieces if bread and this caused the Beri-Beri to transfer from my feet to my stomach within hours and I was in awful pain. I cut out the bread and was soon well again and taking more caution on eating anything bulky.

Our sleeping quarter were below deck in the hold of the ship in hammocks. In spite of not being used to hammocks I slept soundly until next morning. The conditions on board were so comfortable in comparison with what we had become accustomed to that we imagined we were on a pleasure cruise. That was before we knew about the existence of an Officer Commanding Troops. This is an Army Officer who takes overall charge of Army Personnel aboard a troopship at sea.

Some men were put onto mess duties and various cleaning tasks, I was ordered to go on anti-submarine watch on deck at ten o'clock that night. I duly reported at a meeting place and three of us were taken to a place on the fore deck and told to keep watch for submarines. This was in the dark and with the naked eye. We had been at our post for some two hours and it started to blow and rain.

A Ships Officer appeared and said, "Who are you men and what are you doing out here in this weather?" We said rather lamely that we were watching for submarines. The Naval Officer replied "Who the hell sent you here?" "The O.C. Troops" we replied. "What Regiment are you from?" "We are ex-prisoners of war" I explained. "I am the Captain of this ship, you men are not to be given any duties." He turned to his Orderly, "Take these men down to the Mess Room and see they get some cocoa and anything else they want." He wished us good luck and we went away for our cocoa and hoped he would really give the O.C. Troops a rollicking. There were no more night watches for us. We spent many hours into the early morning playing Bragg or Solo .

Our first port of call was Columbo and as soon as we stepped ashore we were welcomed by most of the European residents and Naval people. The Services had organised some Wrens to entertain us and show us around Columbo. We split into small parties of three or four and had tea with our hosts. We had to be back on the ship by early evening but it was very nice to have some female company after nearly four years without them.

Our next stop was Bombay when we were allowed ashore for three hours. This didn't allow us much time for sight seeing but we were anxious to get home anyway.

It was now getting near the end of September and the only clothes we had were tropical khaki drill. We docked at a place on the Suez Canal route called Adabaya and went ashore to a barracks with many Italian prisoners, where we were fitted out with a full issue of winter Army clothing, enough to last us another two years.

We had picked up mail at Suez some of which was recent but most was up to a year old. Some letter told sons of deaths of their parents perhaps a year ago and in some cases the whole family killed in bombing raids. After all that had sustained them through the last years was the thought of going home to their family. The news left them devastated and their grief had to be in public. Many men had not received any letters since leaving home. This applied particularly to members of 18th Division who had been captured within a few days of landing in Singapore .

It was the first week in October when we arrived in Liverpool Docks. The noise within the shipyards was terrific. Every ships siren was going and the flags were flying to welcome us home. The thought ran through my head - we lost Singapore I wonder what the reception would have been like if we had won.

Out at sea the ships Captain had been told that there was a strike on in Liverpool Docks but the Dockers offered to help us with our baggage off the ship. This offer was refused and we carried all our own baggage off the ship. There were trucks waiting to take us to a camp at Maghull outside Liverpool. The main streets of the town were packed and all the traffic had come to a standstill as we slowly drove through the densely packed streets and with many people trying to shake our hands. All those responsible for our reception including the Red Cross and the Army and Navy had done a wonderful job.

Many of us had put on weight during the voyage and by the time we reached Liverpool we were looking fairly well. had these people seen us when we embarked at Singapore six weeks before they would have been shocked .

We finally reached the reception camp. We were put through medical tests, documentation, pay, leave warrants and questions as to where we wanted to go. This was necessary as many men did not know where their families were. We were then ushered into a beautifully decorated hut by the Red Cross ladies. There were tables with lots of sandwiches, tea with sugar and milk and other luxuries on the tables. There was not room for the lovely cream cakes, doughnuts and other sweets that the Red Cross and other organisations had gathered for us on the tables so they were put on other tables behind us.

After the long voyage we were now able to eat most things and cakes were not on the ships menu. We were looking forward to the sweets when we had attacked the sandwiches. However, there were a lot of Press Reporters and Photographers interviewing and taking pictures. When all the Press hassle had stopped I looked across at the cake tables and was horrified to see many of the Pressmen pulling paper bags from their pockets and stuffing them with our cakes and bolting through the doors. However, we managed one each in the end so we did not bother murdering them.

The tea over, we were again put into trucks and taken to some brick built huts. My kit bag and all I possessed had been put on the wrong truck and I had no more than I stood up in to take home. The hut was bereft of any furniture, beds, tables or boards and some of the windows had no glass in. There was no heating and the door would not shut. It was now about two in the morning and after telling the driver to try and find my kit bag we all lay down on the concrete and went to sleep. We had no lights or matches so we just had to wait for the next morning when someone came to take us to breakfast.

My kit bag turned up the next day for which I was very grateful. Trucks were going to various areas and it was up to each man to find the truck which would take him nearest to his home. I let the driver drop me off at the end of my road as it was a cul de sac and he would not have been able to turn round. I was supposed to have gone straight to the local Council Office where there was a reception committee waiting to welcome me.

However, the wife was at home when I got there and I did get a full bottle of beer two or three days later which was a local homecoming present from Wilmslow District Council.

I was sad to hear of the deaths of so many of my friends in various battle fields throughout the world. I had heard of the massacre at Alexander Hospital in Singapore and of the killing of a doctor there, but it was not until I arrived home that I found he was a member of our Rugby Club.

It seemed that "Survival was for Me".